The Serfitt & Cloye Gift Catalog

JUST ENOUGH OF TOO MUCH

BOB WOODIWISS *with illustrations by Andrea Jensen*

TOW BOOKS
Cincinnati, Ohio
www.towbooks.com

A LETTER FROM OUR PRESIDENT

To our esteemed clientele

In late 1908, exactly one hundred years ago, my grandfather, Franklin Deuteronomy Serfitt, along with his good friend and business partner Artemis Mitchell Parker Cloye, mailed out the first ever catalog of supra-upscale merchandise: the Serfitt & Cloye Christmas Compendium of Immoderation. It was created to make available to the world's economic aristocracy the most extraordinary goods the mind of man could conceive and the hand of man produce. Inside were items of unprecedented quality, originality, exclusivity, sophistication, and magnificence. And if, overall, the prices excluded persons who were merely excessively comfortable, Grandfather was entirely comfortable with that.

Through this revolutionary new catalog, patrician, monopolist, and industrial baron alike could favor himself with gifts of grandeur (Archduke Franz Ferdinand's jewel-encrusted handlebar mustache) and novelty (the first true computer, a coal-fired machine with the sole function of automatically calculating how much coal it was burning), of refinement (a Bugatti Type 10 with full-time onboard indentured cartographer/navigation system) and rusticity (over five hundred lost tintypes of Appalachian hillbilly erotica photographed by Mathew Brady).

And favor themselves they did. Wholeheartedly. By the time the New Year was rung in, Serfitt & Cloye had firmly established itself as the world's foremost purveyor of sybaritic indulgery. The first true LuxuRetailer®.

Much has changed since then, of course. The world today is one of overabundance and overpopulation, of mass production and spot-on knockoffs, of emulation and astronomical preapproved credit limits. More simply put, there are more people, more goods, and more money in the marketplace. Making it harder and harder for anyone—even you!—to find, much less possess, something truly unique, something you alone can enjoy without fear of someone else having or knowing that exact same enjoyment.

Yet the fact remains, you desire such objects. Require and demand them. Can afford them. Which is why Serfitt & Cloye has not changed. And never will.

On these pages, for the hundredth consecutive year, you'll once again encounter the latest, the smartest, the chicest, the most uncommon and least unextraordinary goods, services, and life enhancements available anywhere. Here, nothing is beyond the imagination, because nothing is beyond your grasp.

Best of the season,

F.D. "Trip" Serfitt III

F.D. "Trip" Serfitt III
Chairman
Serfitt & Cloye

P.S. Throughout this year's catalog, to commemorate our centenary, we've reprinted some memorable gifts from Christmases past. We hope you enjoy this trip down Memory Boulevard.

THE SERFITT & CLOYE MISSION: To consistently offer the deserving few who have amassed the greatest fiscal success, through venerable birthright and/or towering achievement, with the opportunity to indulge their voluptuous tastes to an extent commensurate with their assets.

THE SERFITT & CLOYE PHILOSOPHY

The $75,000-per-year bank executive drives a luxury automobile that costs $75,000. The $30,000 warehouse worker owns a $40,000 boat. The homeless woman splurges on a 40-ounce bottle of brand-name beer for $1.49. These three people have indulged themselves at, respectively, 100 percent, 133 percent, and infinity percent of their annual wage. To which we say *mazel tov*.

But what of our most auspicious citizens? Where, for example, is the $31 million treat to match the 2007 annual compensation of Capital One's Richard Fairbank? On what will Warren Buffett spend the $10 billion difference between his 2006 net worth and his 2007 net worth? What can Larry Ellison possibly buy his children that will prove he's willing to sacrifice anything for them? Shouldn't this land of equality afford such venerable achievers a proportionate slice of the amenity pie?

Serfitt & Cloye thinks so. That's why we make no apologies for the extravagant items we offer or the prices they command. (And why you should feel pride in your purchases.) The longstanding, ongoing, and appalling luxury imbalance deserves to be and shall be eradicated. Please, let's shop till it drops.

THE SERFITT & CLOYE GUARANTEE

Serfitt & Cloye has every expectation that the items contained in this catalog will be free of defect and will appear, perform, and endure exactly as described. Similarly, we are confident that the procedures and services offered herein will be performed with an almost irritating attention to detail and completed to your total satisfaction. We are, in fact, so convinced of the superior quality of everything we sell, we will, upon receipt of your verified complaint, retain outside counsel, file suit against ourselves, and aggressively pursue legal and financial redress from us on your behalf.

Serfitt & Cloye

Where opulence lives in luxury.

www.serfittandcloye.com

Perpetual Puppy

Christmas morning. Bright and early. Your doorbell rings. It's FedEx, delivering to you the cutest, bounciest, heart-stealingest 8-week-old pedigreed puppy you've ever seen. Of course, puppy loves to cuddle and frolic. Like any puppy. But unlike "any puppy," yours will never grow into a big, disappointing, troublesome lump of a dog. That's because the very next morning—and every morning throughout your contract period—a new, 8-week-old cloned duplicate puppy will be delivered to your door, and your "old," already-less-cute, 8-week-and-1-day-old puppy will be whisked covertly away. The transition is seamless. Painless. And your pup never grows up. Show-quality bloodlines. Available in Golden Retriever, King Charles Spaniel, Lhasa Apso, and four sizes of poodle. ***Perpetual Puppy (6-month contract): $599,000; Perpetual Puppy (1-year contract): $999,000; Perpetual Puppy (5-year contract): $4.5 million.***

Patek Philippe Timeless Watch

Meetings don't start until you get there. The Gulfstream doesn't take off until you're seat-belted and champagned. You don't make reservations, you cause unprepared maître d's to fawn to the point of self-loathing. More simply put, you can never be late because nothing can start without you. That's why the Patek Philippe Timeless Watch has a clean, uncluttered, unadorned face. *Without* hour, minute, or sweep second hands. This uniquely styled nonchronometer lets you and those around you know with just a glimpse of the wrist that you don't need to be anywhere right now but precisely where you are. Handsomely styled in your choice of brushed or polished solid platinum ingot, the no-hands design permits the watch face to be set with over 25 carats of flawless brilliant-cut diamonds, each large enough to kiss the inside surface of the sapphire crystal. Hours are marked by Roman numerals scrupulously sculpted by Florentine stone carvers from rock collected from the lunar surface by Apollo 11 astronauts. And no spring, quartz, tourbillon, or other internal movements means far fewer repairs than with traditional timekeeping timepieces. Water resistant and fully nonfunctional to unlimited ocean depths. ***Timeless Watch: $1.3 million.***

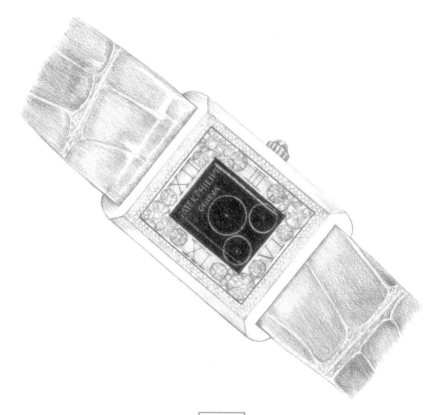

Architectural Digest Parking Space

One doesn't own a car in Manhattan without also owning a parking space to put it in. And while, yes, it is possible to find a conveniently located, perfectly serviceable midtown space in the $200,000 range, such slots are normally bland, disappointing fixer-uppers, hardly fitting for a hand-assembled, road-carving Italian racing coupe or a custom-crafted, monarch-worthy British luxury coach. No, the truly pampered car deserves the amenities and appointments of our *Architectural Digest* Parking Space. This highly practical triple-wide, double-long space accommodates parallel, perpendicular, and diagonal parking, always with ample room for doors to swing fully open for fluid cabin entry and exit. The 17th-century silk Persian area rug provides a serene, supple surface to pull onto, muting tire noise and passively wiping treads clean. A quartet of Tiffany floor lamps casts soft light that brings out the prole-rubbed luster of multiple paint coats. A capacious George III marquetry-inlaid credenza offers abundant storage space for any tools and materials one's detailer may require. Finally, a graceful I.M. Pei carport sublimely shelters and safeguards its treasured tenant from the elements and features the same theft- and vandal-thwarting security system used to protect American embassies in Islamic countries. **Architectural Digest Parking Space: $25.5 million.**

iLozenge

For nosher and gourmand alike, the Apple iLozenge puts up to 10,000 of your favorite flavors at your taste bud tips. This fully functional post-beta, pre-production prototype is a product of bleeding-edge nanotechnology, a Life Saver–sized 4-terabyte device that allows the user to download delicious, spot-on flavors via Apple's iSuck (intranet) Web site. Simply fill the "flavor player" with your desired selections, choose (via voice-activated interface) the dish or foodstuff you're craving, pop the iLozenge in your mouth, and get ready for heaping gigabytes of gastronomic delight. The iLozenge's gustatory reproduction is 99.4% accurate across the entire taste spectrum (salty, sweet, sour, bitter, and savory), individually or in combination. So "Salt" tastes shaker fresh, "Le Canard à la Presse" tastes just ducky. And since iLozenge's flavors are digital, there are no calories, there is no loss of intensity over time, and there is no garlic (or onion or anything else) breath. On the iSuck Web site, you'll find complex signature dishes from three-star Michelin restaurants; earthy ethnic cuisines; full fast-food menus; countless brand-name frozen and prepared meals, snacks, and candies; as well as niche and novelty foods (like shark fin soup and shark fin soup crackers). *The iLozenge: $279,000. Required ultra-highspeed (50GB/second) Internet connection (per month): $595. iSuck flavors (per download): $999.99.*

Lancôme/Northrop Grumman Obscurifying Facial Serum

Dr. Rodney Cohn, a cosmetic technologist, took a novel approach to the issue of aging: What if "old" isn't how one *appears*, but how one is *perceived*? It was this radical reframing that allowed Dr. Cohn to move beyond the false hope of age-defying creams to the true miracle of age-deflecting cream. The difference? This lightly fragrant, easy-to-apply emulsion isn't formulated to moisturize or exfoliate or smooth one's skin—because, as any reputable dermatologist will tell you, all efforts to stop or slow the ravages of time are a waste of time. Instead, Obscurifying Facial Serum—developed by the scientists behind the stealth bomber—is rich in microscopic, microfaceted, microrefracting particles designed to absorb, deflect, and disperse specific portions of the light spectrum, thus preventing their observation and perception by the human eye. So when you rub this Serum into your fine-line wrinkles or deep skin creases, they don't go away, they simply can't be seen. They're blurred and erased not off your face, but simply in the eyes of others. Try it. And embrace the difference between looking younger and being seen as younger. *Lancôme/Northrop Grumman Obscurifying Facial Serum (1-ounce bottle): $50,000.*

Nesting Elton John Outfits

The whimsy and artistry of Russian nesting dolls is the inspiration behind this clever collectible, a fusion of art, fashion, stagecraft, and resplendent homosexuality. Here, seven separate stage outfits worn by the legendary performer Sir Elton John are all neatly nestled one inside the other. You'll love the outermost *couture* (a sequin-and-sateen Beefeater uniform in lime green) from his bulkiest, flamingest incarnation (2005), but that's just the candy shell. As you peel away layer after layer of one outrageous costume after another, it's "Goodbye Yellow Brick Road," Hello, Memory Lane. Because each ensemble is a tad trimmer, a soupçon less flamboyant. Until finally, deep inside, you've returned to 1969, when the pop icon's fame was nascent, his frame slender, his tastes closeted, and faded blue jeans paired with a silk-screened gray tee-shirt were enough to charm his fans. Display the outfits fully nested, or disassemble and display them separately in a descending or ascending sequence. *Nesting Elton John Outfits: $28 million. (One Madame Tussaud–quality Elton John mannequin is included. Six additional mannequins, in broadening physiques, for displaying costumes individually are available for an additional $3 million.)*

Many an impassioned and cogent argument has been made in support of capital punishment over the years, but none is quite so eloquent, so beautiful, so practical as Texas Tableware by Wedgwood. This exquisitely crafted fine bone china is a limited-edition 140-piece service for 20 (plus serving pieces) made from the bone ash of all 400 prisoners executed by the Texas Department of Criminal Justice since that state resumed the death penalty in 1982. The felonious bones—sold to us by the state as valuable assets of the deceased evildoers, with all proceeds being equally distributed to their victims' funds—were calcined at temperatures in excess of 1,000° Celsius, giving the executed even more of what they surely deserved. The ash was then mixed with china clay, shaped, and kiln-fired at a soul-purifying 1,250° Celsius. The china's pattern—a platinum chain girding the edges, a gold and platinum avenging angel in the center—is applied by hand, as is the final glaze. The finished pieces radiate a delicate luminosity that belies the hard, dark men that went into them. Ladies and gentlemen, dinner and justice are served. *Texas Tableware: $5.75 million.*

Go-F**k-Yourself Pumps

It's been well over a decade since the introduction of the last great "message shoe," the provocative and popular come-f**k-me pump. But the high-flying, coke-fueled eighties are long gone, and you've matured, become less lusting, grown more scorning. Now, you've got a brand new message to send. And these, by gadfry, are just the shoes to do it. Go-F**k-Yourself Pumps by Manolo Blahnik are the first footwear to summarily dismiss pick-up artists, suitors, gigolos, trawlers, horn dogs, drunks, and the unfortunately unattractive—all from far across a room, before they ever approach. A single glance at your GFYPs, at their precise angle and height, at their low-gloss patina and muted color palette, at their menacingly sharp steel-clad toes and faux-blood-stained soles, clues in even the cluelessest swain: Go F**k Yourself, little man. You'll save time, money, and a world of trouble by giving guys the big pre-kiss-off. Besides, could there be a happier way to break your man habit than with your shoe habit? *Go-F**k-Yourself Pumps: $100,000.*

Pore-Swabbing

Ask any holistic healer: The first step toward achieving inner peace is a thorough outer cleansing. Yet the seaweed wraps, the green coffee wraps, the salt glows, the herbal soaks and teas so common at common spas and resorts do only a passable job of purification and detoxification. Not so pore-swabbing. This recently revived ancient Japanese treatment/sacred ceremony is a meticulous, painstaking, pleasure-inducing swabbing of each of your skin's millions of individual pores. Our skilled, sterilized team of twelve Skin Divers® wields single slender Egyptian cotton fibers tipped with a purifying, rejuvenating lavender aloe scrub to softly purge pores *one at a time*. Beneath their swift hands and intense, spiritual focus, you'll attain a hitherto unimagined cutaneous clarity. A clarity that will awaken in you the divine knowledge that you're not fully clean until you're Zenfully clean. ***Pore-Swabbing: $2.3 million (includes private air transportation and one-week spa accommodations in Kyoto, Japan).***

Flauntable Folding Money

Anyone who's ever paid cash for an item can attest to this: Money is boring. Dullsville. Yours is exactly like everyone else's. Same size, same shape, same color, same denominations. It's no different than if the whole world was driving the same year, model, and color Maybach as you; or if everyone inseminated their mares with the same Triple Crown winner's semen. It's practically communistic to contemplate! New Flauntable Folding Money, however, takes the tedium out of your money clip and stuffs it with bills rarer than rare coins. Each note features your portrait in a unique, commissioned work of art you'll be proud to flash. That informs the world you won't settle for the same old, same cold cash. An embedded microchip on each bill identifies it as legal tender the world over. And the boring change merchants give back? Well, there's always recycling. *Flauntable Folding Money (packet of a hundred $250 bills): $2.5 million. Ask about our custom denominations (20% upcharge).*

Lagerfeld Triple Reversible Coat

Leave it to the provocative Karl Lagerfeld to create the first garment ever to uncover and exploit the creative possibilities of a hitherto theoretical dimension. All three facets (inside, outside, and unside) of this spectacular, inimitable piece of outerwear are so skillfully realized and magnificently styled that deciding which one to flaunt next promises to be a nearly impossible task. First, for sheer elegance, there's a boldly imagined, impeccably executed overcoat woven from 100% vicuña wool. Reverse it and you reveal a sumptuous calf-length Russian sable coat tailored to show off as well as enhance your every advantage. Reverse it yet again and it's a 50/50 cashmere-antineutrino blend jacket that is immune to the laws of gravity, facilitates communication with the dead, and exists simultaneously in the Pleistocene era. Size 0 only. *Lagerfeld Triple Reversible Coat: $1 billion.*

Martha Stewart's International Space Station Adventure

The ultimate learning vacation. Just you (or your lucky gift-getter) and decorating goddess/diva—and socioeconomic peer—Martha Stewart alone together for three full weeks, high above Earth in the solar system's only manned (or, rather, "womaned") space station. You'll work and live closely with, assist, get tips from, zero gravitate alongside, and nearly get to know America's übertastemaker as you team up to lighten, brighten, and cozy this dingy outpost in the vastness of space. (Preshipped materials reveal that the interior is to be redecorated in a French country kitchen motif, with exposed-beam ceiling and cornflower blue and mustard yellow color scheme.) You'll also learn to make and imaginatively serve twenty-five Tang-based desserts and cocktails. An Extra-vehicular Activity Excursion puts you and Martha in Prada spacesuits as you head outside to carry out exterior enhancements, including a modular gazebo. Vodka reception with cosmonauts on docking, after which they return to Earth in your spacecraft. *Martha Stewart's International Space Station Adventure: $85 million.*

Breakfast Beyond Tiffany's

It's said that breakfast is the most important meal of the day. Chef François Lucre, however, will turn it into the most important meal of your life. At your convenience, M. Lucre and his staff shall prepare a pair of the most fabulous omelets in the history of the culinary arts. He'll begin with 24 billion Beluga caviar eggs, each individually hand-cracked and the yolks retained. The eggs will then be impeccably, exotically herbed, whisked, and, over a low flame, patiently firmed and lightly browned in butter churned from the milk of humpback whales. Just before folding, each omelet will be stuffed with 6 ounces of that rarest of breakfast meats, panda fetus pancetta, a delicate delight that the ancient Chinese twice went to war for and that has been unavailable in the West since the Endangered Species Act (not enforced in the international waters where M. Lucre shall be preparing your meal). Lightly salted by the chef's tears of triumph, garnished with a single sprig of Italian parsley cultivated in the dirt collected from under the fingernails of 34 former presidents. Forbiddenly delicious. ***Breakfast Beyond Tiffany's: $9.9 million. (Gratuity separate. Toast, juice, and coffee optional.)***

OUR SOURCES

Every product and service contained in this catalog is offered exclusively by Serfitt & Cloye. Many are one-of-a-kind items. Not surprisingly, given the depth, breadth, and acclamation of what we sell, we're often asked where our gift items come from. In reply, we can only say that our sources are as diverse as the offerings themselves.

• **Our buyers.** This dedicated group of eagle-eyed treasure hawks is constantly circling the globe—and in some cases the solar system—for the exotic and the unusual, always keeping in mind that, for the right *objet*, money is no *objet*.

• **Privately and publicly owned corporations.** When a business finds that a high-concept product or service in which it has already invested heavily is unfeasible or impossible to cost-effectively mass produce or deliver, it turns to the one and only retailer capable of turning market miscalculations into gold: Serfitt & Cloye.

• **Subcontracted manufacturers.** Our extensive worldwide network of skilled, reliable companies and individual artisans has time and again proven it can and will produce the highest quality products from our detailed specifications, and do it with a laudably amoral approach and invaluable indifference to the methods or consequences of procuring the raw materials and/or the requisite labor.

• **Other sources.** The original ideas behind many Serfitt & Cloye goods and services have their genesis with equally far-ranging sources, including: secretaries and assistants to the world's elite who, desperate to satisfy their employers' "unrealistic" requests and demands, phone our headquarters looking for help; ideation sessions with nontraditional outside-the-box thinkers, such as opium eaters, the institutionalized, and those experiencing fever dreams; druids and necromancers; classic comics and Tom Swift books; and the purloined doodle pads of Thomas Pynchon.

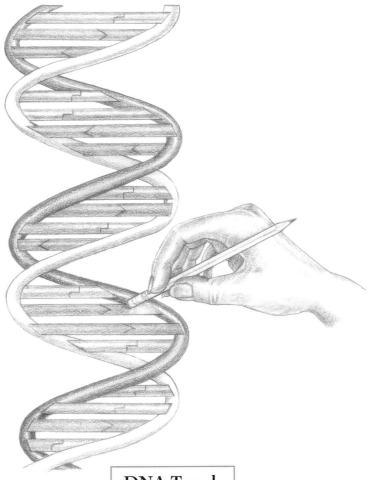

DNA Tweak

Imagine, just for the sake of argument, you've committed a felony. And even though you've retained some best-that-money-can-buy lawyer, you know you're going down. All because of some incontrovertible DNA evidence. Or should we say *formerly* incontrovertible? Because with this patented new process developed by EffiGenome, your DNA can be modified, altered, or mutated a vital soupçon. Just enough to keep it from matching any blood residue or tissue samples found at the crime scene. Yet everything else about you will remain you—there are absolutely no physical or mental ramifications, now or ever (signed responsibility waiver required; one-year limited warranty). DNA Tweaks are also effective for beating paternity suits, disinheriting displeasing adult children, refuting claims of being fellated by a White House intern, and more. Performed at EffiGenome Labs in Palo Alto, California, the procedure is nonsurgical, noninvasive, nondrowsy. Valet parking is included. ***DNA Tweak: $10 million. (Insurance not accepted.)***

Fab Fur Toilet Tissue

What could be more sumptuous, more soothing, more splendidly sensual than the feel of fur? Certainly not pulped and rolled paper products. Now, experience the uniquely tactile tingle of skins on skin whenever you feel the urge. The urge to relieve yourself, that is. With Fab Fur Toilet Tissue, evacuation is merely a prelude to delicious sensation. Decadently absorbent. Almost shamefully cleansing. An absolutely *un*domesticated pleasure. Each Fab Fur square is center cut from top quality farm-raised pelts, never trims and ends. It's a return to nature every time nature calls. Choose from classic mink, lustrous sable, luxuriant beaver, or chichi chinchilla. Two-ply (fur on both front and back) double rolls. *Fab Fur Toilet Tissue (box of 48): $350,000.*

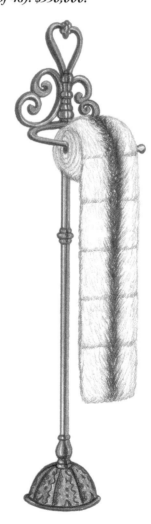

Rational Exuberance

Look at you sitting there with but a single cup instead of a whole pot, with nylonless legs, and—oh, dear!—shoes from two seasons ago. The worst part is, you're giving Hitler and his henchman exactly what they want. That's right. That bristle-lipped lamebrain is over the moon that this country's most affluent and influential families are scraping by on stingy rations, sacrificing, doing without. Because he knows that by bringing you low, reducing you to the common man's level, he demoralizes the thousands—the tens of thousands—who look to you as all that's right with and attainable in America. Well, by golly, it's time to spit in the Fatherland's unmonocled eye—without hurting the war effort. We're making available to you and you alone every single ration book from every single patriotic citizen in Elko, Nevada—a town of 3,000—for the next year. With these coupons, you'll return to your old life of buttered everything and a bottomless tank of gasoline to pick up more. Plus, you'll have the satisfaction of knowing your consumption is inspiring the nation and making a certain Kraut sour. ***Rational Exuberance: $2.25 million.***

Fictionalization

For anyone who's ever dreamed of being a character in a Jane Austen novel. For the fiction lover who feels that in reading Yossarian's, Gatsby's, Karenina's, or Portnoy's story that she is reading her own. For the person who always thought she'd pour her heart into the creation of a great book one day, but now knows there's a faster, easier way. Yes, for all these literature lovers and more, may we suggest Fictionalization. With Fictionalization, you give the gift of fictional life. Because your name (or the name of whomever you should choose to designate) will replace the name of your favorite fictional character throughout any classic, near-classic, or pulp novel. Name substitution will begin with a newly published edition that will replace all existing editions and shall continue in perpetuity, that is, *in all subsequent printings of your selected title for all time*. Demand is already hot, so make your reservation now. Titles already in production include Flaubert's *Madame Winfrey*, Burroughs's *Murdoch of the Apes*, and Shakespeare's *Rosie O['Donnell] & Juliet*. Hundreds of other titles available. ***Fictionalization: from $100,000 (Friar Tuck level) to $100 million (Jesus Christ level).***

No one likes to feel weak, helpless. And let's face it, all those bodyguards and personal assistants on the payroll can exacerbate rather than alleviate the problem. So Adrenaline 24/7 provides users with superhuman strength all day, every day, in every situation. Far faster than working out, far safer than steroids. This refillable reservoir of pure human adrenaline is mounted in a discreet body cavity and taps directly into the bloodstream via sterile stent. Now, you can lift a car not just in the rare emergency of it being atop your child, but also to efficiently, effortlessly clear it from a plum parking space. Insulted by a passerby? Don't send your bodyguards and give the brash ruffian the satisfaction of thinking you're a cowardly pantywaist; pick him up and chuck him like a javelin. Oh, yeah! You'll have so much *physical* strength you may never choose to negotiate from a position of *financial* strength again! Includes body cavity assessment, custom body cavity reservoir, stent, all associated medical procedures, and 30-day supply of pure human adrenaline. *Adrenaline 24/7: $4.5 million. (Additional adrenaline packs available separately. Not responsible for mood swings or ringing in ears.)*

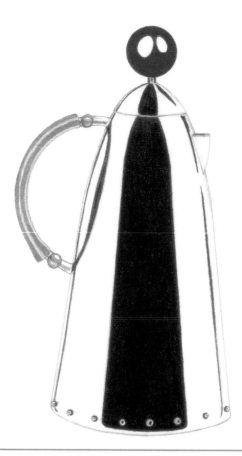

Serfitt & Cloye *Eau Fraîche* Synthesizer

Pure bottled water? Pure fiction. Consider: The Alpine snows that yield Evian are, in fact, a toilet for countless bird and animal species. And the aquifer at Fiji's source may, as claimed, filter out pollutants, but it can't sanitize the swarthy, sweaty island worker who bottles it. Truth is, if you're drinking any of today's countless bottled water brands, you may be getting hydrated, but you're also getting hosed. Conversely, the Serfitt & Cloye *Eau Fraîche* Synthesizer makes your water fresh, pure, and on demand, and it never runs dry. The source of this wellspring? The Integrated Gas Interfusion Chamber housed in the oversized cap atop the Synthesizer's Michael Graves–designed 32-ounce insulated titanium carafe. Inside this sophisticatedly simple thermonuclear chamber, hydrogen and oxygen that are continuously extracted from the air are united, two plump *H*s and one juicy *O* at a time, into clear, pristine, thirst-quenching molecules of water. Brand spanking new water. Unsullied by chemicals or pollutants of any kind. Untouched at any stage by sweaty Fijians, filthy Frenchmen, or even drunk Canadians. Refreshing, yes? Produces approximately 8 ounces of water/hour. ***The Serfitt & Cloye* Eau Fraîche *Synthesizer: $99,000.***

Sprinkling *Avec Gaz* System

In your quest for the lushest, thickest, greenest lawn, you can only throw so many fertilizers, pesticides, and Japanese gardeners at it. Then you either have to accept their limitations, or kill it ... with kindness, we mean. Sprinkling *Avec Gaz* is a new way, a better way, to water your lawn. Because this is the only watering system to use Perrier, the naturally carbonated water from the south of France. When soaked with Perrier, your lawn not only receives a pure, unprocessed drink of life-giving H_2O, it also gets a bubbly burst of revitalizing CO_2. You water, feed, and aerate all at the same time. Before you know it, your lawn is as distinctively green as the bottle its water is famous for. Includes automatic sprinkler system, installation (up to 1 acre of lawn), 25,000-gallon underground reservoir, and 25,000 gallons of Perrier (delivered). ***Sprinkling Avec Gaz System: $400,000. Refills: $250,000.***

You're committed to higher education. The endowed chairs and campus buildings bearing your family name are testament to that. Still, you want to do more. You want to make a real and lasting difference in the lives of young people. You want to inspire them. Expose them to the imperatives of achievement. And what could be more instructive than the life and times, the actions and examples of one of the world's most successful citizens: You. You-ology is a forthcoming fully accredited degree program that will not merely be named for you, but be all *about* you. By our exclusive arrangement, Harvard University, America's most respected institution of higher learning, will establish a field of study on the subject of you, compiling a core curriculum and research library that comprehensively cover every aspect of your existence, from cradle to present to (in time) grave/cryogenic chamber. Students will explore and study topics as diverse as your accomplishments, your philosophy, your decency, your humility, and your pets. Undergraduate, graduate, and doctoral degrees will be offered. ***You-ology Program: $250 million.***

African-American Fantasy Camp

Is there a special Republican powerbroker in your life you'd like to thank? Maybe an old friend who's been legislating or ruling from the bench on the "right" side—your side!—of every issue? Doubtless there is. And we have just the thing for this hardworking, ambitious, unfairness-fighting white male: a relaxing respite from the high-pressure, high-stakes world he's burdened with ruling. A taste of the sweet life he's so long been denied. A chance to live the dream of being black in America. African-American Fantasy Camp is one full month/welfare cycle in a totally realistic but continuously surveilled urban environment featuring all the advantages of the carefree minority lifestyle: The entitlements and preferential treatment. The lazy days on sunny street corners with nowhere to be. The flaunting of the law. The warm, demonstrative mother. The innate cool. The sympathetic portrayal by the left-wing media. The uninhibited use of the N-word without legal or social repercussions. This is the ultimate reward for those who've been trapped too long on the inside looking out. African-American Fantasy Camp—where the livin' is easy. Package includes skin tinting injections and reversal injections, tenement penthouse crib, phat wardrobe, pimped ride, posse, ho, per diem of chronic and 40s, unlimited "payday loans" at a low introductory 36% weekly interest rate. *African-American Fantasy Camp: $825,000.*

Papal Quality Crucifix Necklace

Were it simply a piece of art jewelry, this stunning necklace would be coveted by the few who would dare afford it. But when one considers that it is also a tangible expression of how much one values Jesus Christ, the Son of God, it transcends earthly assessment and enters another, more heavenly realm. In physical detail, the crucifix consists of a slender mahogany cross exquisitely carved from the cabriole leg of an early 18th-century Chippendale chair; the affixed body of the Lord is artisan-cast from the smelted golden scepter of Nefertiti (circa 1338 B.C.); finally, the figure is inlaid with the most flawless of gems, harvested from the crown jewels of no fewer than six deposed monarchies: sapphire "eyes," emerald "thorns," ruby "drops of blood" and "nail heads." Styled as a pendant, this stunning crucifix hangs from an understated 18-inch linen cord woven from strands unraveled from the perimeter of the Shroud of Turin and strung with 33 one-carat diamonds, one for each glorious year of the Christian Savior's short but eventful life. Rated "Sublime" by the Vatican Council. *Papal Quality Crucifix Necklace: $500 million.*

Non-Bobble Head

The ultimate sports fanatic deserves the ultimate sports collectible. And we've got it: Hall of Famer Ted Williams's frozen head. Obtained through his estate, this one-of-a-kind collector's item comes in its own shatterproof Plexiglas cryogenic display case. The left-fielder's eyes are open, his hair is neatly combed, his jaw freshly shaved; the entire head is perfectly preserved, thoroughly lifelike, and in pristine condition. Put Ted's head in the front entry hall to greet guests. Or in the den so you can "watch" the game together. But wherever you put the Splendid Splinter, rest assured, you're batting 1.000 in the Major Memorabilia League. ***Non-Bobble Head: $100 million. (Coming soon for movie buffs: Walt Disney's frozen head.)***

Bad News Well Read

Bombs detonating. Natural disasters. Death and disease. A plunge in the Dow. No new tax cuts in sight. Every day, the newspapers—maybe the newspapers in the very chain you own—are full of depressing, devastating stories. Leaving you with a choice: Start your day off with a downer, or remain happy but uninformed. Enter choice number 3: Bad News Well Read. BNWR is an audio edition of the complete *New York Times*—every page of every section—as read by the cast and characters of *The Simpsons* and delivered to your radio or computer daily via private audio link. Never before has the news, no matter how grim, seemed so light-hearted. Hear Homer describe the homeless orphans of the Darfur genocide. Get Bart's spin on the Iraq insurgency. And laugh like mad at Doctor Nick's obituaries. Turns every distressing page into the funny pages. ***Bad News Well Read (1-year subscription): $700 million. (Also available: the* Times *[of London] read by the surviving members of* Monty Python's Flying Circus; *the* Moscow Times *read by the You Will Now Laugh Heartily, People comedy troupe; and* USA Today *read by the former cast of* Hee Haw.)**

1963

Blast of Freedom

Classless society? Common ownership of the means of production? Rise of the proletariat? What can the Communists be thinking? If their philosophy weren't so galling, it would be laughable. But you're not laughing. Especially given the recent troubles down Cuba way. That got you thinking: Should the Russkies launch and win a nuclear exchange with the United States, you could be left with very little—or worse, the same as everyone else. So how about teaching them a little something before your assets are obliterated and you're assigned to a reeducation camp? Blast of Freedom makes that possible. By putting your finger on the button that will launch the first U.S. nuclear missile over the Iron Curtain. In the event of a confrontation, you'll be whisked to a missile silo at an undisclosed location and assigned your ready station. Then, should the brinksmanship go over the brink, you'll get the order to "Fire!" Later, as the few remaining Muscovites step over the countless dead and stagger, dazed, around the rubble of their city wondering what hit them, you'll know it was you. And regardless of what happens after that—win, lose, or draw—you'll know you struck a blow for freedom as well as for your supremely American way of life. *Blast of Freedom: $1 million.*

Sure, you benefited disproportionately from the Bush tax cuts, but so did all your friends. And though the estate tax repeal would, if passed, be a boon to your family, it would do no more for you than for a couple hundred other families. Don't you think it's time you *and you alone* got something from this country you give so much to? We do. And we've got the votes to make it happen. In committee and on the floors of both Congressional chambers. So whether your legislative necessity is personal, professional, or preposterous, we've got an amendment (number XXVIII) waiting to be tailored to you. Only you. Will you opt for the establishment of a single legal computer operating system? Outlawing community property? Installing your chef's *coq au vin* as the national bird? A prohibition of the phrase *loudmouth drunk and founder of CNN*? It's completely your call. Just say the word and we'll make it law. This is democracy the way it's supposed to be: Your way. ***Constitutional Amendment: $5 billion.***

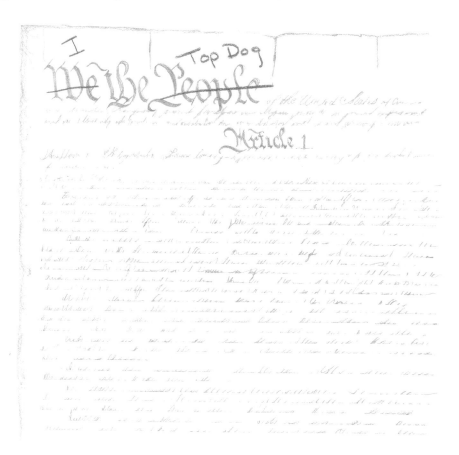

Jungfrau 360-Speed Bike

You don't have to be a serious cyclist to show other cyclists you're more serious about cycling than they can afford to be. All it takes is the Jungfrau 360-Speed Bike. This is the bicycle that shows geography—and everyone on it—who's boss. Because the Jungfrau is topographically unstoppable, tackling and defeating, in ascent and descent, hills, mountains, even sheer cliff faces. With an individual, perfectly calibrated gear for every single degree of inclination, every degree of declination. An automatic derailleur linked to a terrain-reading sensor means the Jungfrau makes perfect shift decisions in real time. Special ultra-sticky, rock-biting tires give you a firm grip on the softest earth or the hardest granite, whether on private property or public parkland. Throw in a carbon-fiber frame and hand-made tubular tires filled with hydrogen, and you have a bike that may not be lighter than air, but is definitely lighter than *theirs*. For reaching the summit, this is the apex. ***Jungfrau 360-Speed Bike (specify touring or trail model): $395,000.***

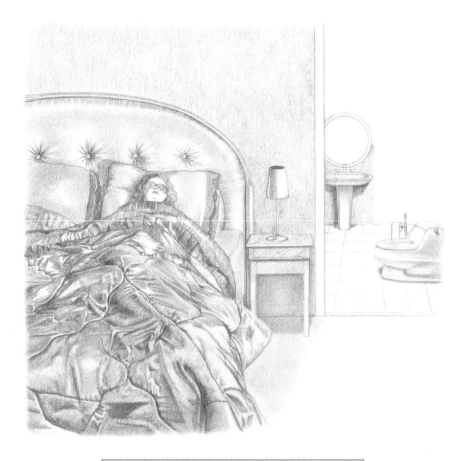

EverRest SuperAbsorbent Bed

It's 3:00 A.M. You're sleeping soundly when … damn, you have to get up and urinate. Or at least you used to. Today, with the EverRest SuperAbsorbent Bed, you can urinate right where you lie. Without urine mess, without urine musk. Because when it comes to handling number 1, the EverRest SuperAbsorbent Bed is number 1. It starts on the outside with a sheath of technical fabric that wicks moisture away from you, the sleeper. Inside the mattress you'll find an accommodating foundation of exceptionally thirsty and comfortably plush fiberfill blended with sumptuously yielding, moisture-resistant swan down, all firmly supported by rustproof stainless steel springs. Finally, the box springs house a whisper-quiet state-of-the-art internal dry-cleaning system that integrates a high-efficiency dehumidification unit with an array of odor neutralizers and air fresheners to keep mold, mildew, and odors at bay. So answer nature's late-night call (or calls) simply, swiftly, horizontally. And relish the youthful luxury of uninterrupted sleep night after night after night. *EverRest SuperAbsorbent Bed: $750,000. InstaDry fabric sheets and pajama bottoms in Satinesque finish sold separately.*

Good Company

We've all heard the old adage: Money can't buy friends. But how about this updated bit of truth: Friends can be really disappointing. Like the pal who hates hospitals and won't visit you there. Or the attention-starved chum who writes a tell-all book about you. And what about your buddy the President, whose loyalty doesn't extend to granting you a full pardon? Friends like that you don't need. And better friends than that, friend, *you can buy*. Good Company offers scores of educated, attractive, discreet people who, on objective, standardized tests, exceed the aggregate scores of randomly sampled "best friends" in areas like loyalty, trust, respect, availability, sycophancy, and echoing your sentiments. All carried out with a faux sincerity you'll swear is the real thing. Hundreds of Good Company companions are available to be put on your exclusive retainer. Just select from our photo catalog. Your circle of dear friends is limited only by what you've budgeted for them. Making the richest man in town *literally* also the richest man in town *figuratively*. ***Good Company: $5 million per friend per year. (Available in alcoholic, enabler, and alcohol-free varieties.)***

Charles Bentley
Conductor
Baritone

Jan Richards
Antique Dealer

MaryAnn Potter
CEO Business Incentives

Catherine Day
Team Leader; Mother

John Hartley
Trust Fund; Alcoholic

George Simmons
CEO TechWerks
Alcoholic

Jane Harvey
VP ProjectHome Interiors
"Love my Vicodin"

HOW OUR PRODUCTS ARE MADE

Order from Serfitt & Cloye and you can be sure every aspect, every material, every detail, every nuance, every intangible of our products is absolutely as it should be.

• **Handcrafted products.** To maintain our unparalleled level of quality, we negotiate exclusive contracts with individual artisans and small, specialized craft guilds, with the (implicit) understanding that should we find it necessary to refuse delivery based on substandard work, it won't be our children who go hungry.

• **Designer goods.** We work closely and personally with the world's most creative, gifted, sensitive fashion designers, architects, artists, et cetera, because you really wouldn't want to.

• **High tech and electronic equipment.** Each device is designed for ease of use, with most having been mastered by lesser primates. Workmanship, engineering, and software (where applicable) is guaranteed for six months or until the next product iteration, whichever comes first.

• **Services.** Service providers are distinguished leaders in their fields, credentialed, certified, licensed, and insured, when possible and practicable. Unless otherwise noted, all medical procedures have been extensively tested on people you don't know in places you'll never go.

Beatles Revenge

Despite Don McLean's tuneful argument otherwise, for any Beatles fan, the day the music died was April 10, 1970, when Paul McCartney announced the Fab Four was finished. This news left millions of fans saddened, and not a few maddened. For the latter, we make this suggestion: Don't get mad, get Yoko. Big time and for all time. Beatles Revenge is a dish served 38 years cold, specially prepared for the woman who not only destroyed the best band ever, but, in the process, broke a generation's heart and extinguished forever its youthful idealism. Serfitt & Cloye is pleased to offer one singularly devoted and vengeful Beatles fan the opportunity to have Yoko Ono condemned to Hell (or its equivalent) for all eternity, made possible by the Company's confidential, binding negotiations with the formal and de facto heads of all major world religions and denominations. Said purchaser will receive a handsomely illuminated Certificate of Damnation signed by each spiritual leader and expertly framed. But this is more than the ultimate payback. Beatles Revenge is a hedge against any celestial meddling by Ms. Ono that might forestall the eventual heavenly mop top reunion you're so looking forward to. Yeah, yeah, yeah! *Beatles Revenge: $29 million.*

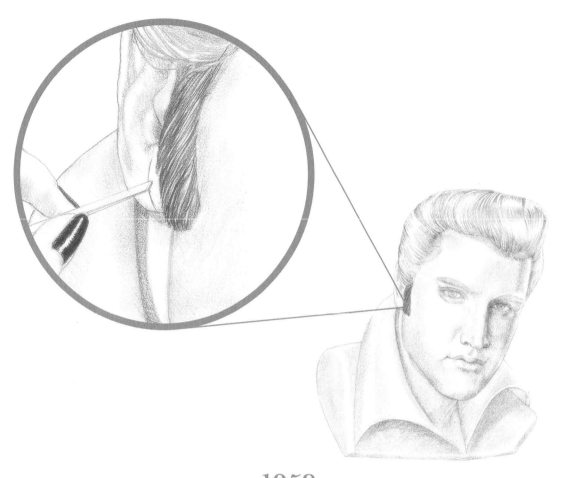

1958
Preserved Presley

Not so many months ago, the world's most popular hip-wiggler, Elvis Presley, was drafted into the U.S. Army. And as countless news photos showed his fans, he received the complimentary shave and haircut that comes with induction. What you may not have seen, however, was the Serfitt & Cloye Sideburn Reclamation Team, a crackerjack crew assembled to faithfully conserve and preserve the rock-and-roll soldier's ear-side embellishments. Pre-shave, the sideburns were photographed from several different perspectives and distances, then each whisker was individually numbered and catalogued; post-shave, the shorn sideburns were collected, hair by hair. Later, in an off-base, sterile, and draftless chamber, the tonsorial process was reversed, and the fully restored lateral facial adornments were affixed to a wax likeness of the preconscripted Presley. If this doesn't get your giddy teenager "All Shook Up," maybe you better give her a good shake. *Preserved Presley: $250,000.*

Enemies and adversaries. They're unavoidable. The cost of doing ruthless business. Sadly, try as one might, not all of them can be immediately crushed, defeated, or assassinated. In the meantime, why not indulge in the next best thing: the symbolic victory afforded through the Ironic Pen. The Ironic Pen is an entirely new way to mock and humiliate those who antagonize one most. Because this pen contains not ink but, rather, the precious, indelible blood of one's enemy. Setting up some deliciously sardonic possibilities. For instance, a defense contractor might sign a lucrative new government contract in Cindy Sheehan's blood. Or a utility's purchase agreement for air pollution credits could be signed in Al Gore's. How about signing your marriage license with O.J.'s circulatory juice? That's ironic gold! When ordering, simply supply the names of up to 10 personal nemeses and we'll do the rest. All blood is quasi-legitimately obtained through our international network of ostensibly licensed physicians and lab technicians. Each sample is accompanied by a certificate of authenticity. Blood comes in 25ml cartridges designed for use with an exquisite Montblanc writing instrument featuring hand-lacquered inlay finish, ergonomic design, and 24-karat gold clot-resistant nib. *Ironic Pen: $7.5 million.*

Cinéma du Jour Grand

Your daughter's wedding. Your son's birth. Your own bachelor(ette) party. Do you really want to entrust such precious memories to on-the-fly "home video" or a low-end professional hack with embarrassing production values and no feel for the arc of your exceptional story? Please. Allow Serfitt & Cloye to arrange for your milestone events to be translated to film by the most talented, most respected, most passionate *auteurs* working today. These visionary artistes will megalomaniacally guide, interpret, and take ownership of your personal story, from pre-pro to post-score. Simply choose a genre—drama, action, comedy, or documentary—then sit back and wait for the magic. Everything—script, locations, color palette, shooting, editing, music rights, you name it—will be professionally carried out in the finest Hollywood tradition. Often on schedule. Ninety days after production wraps, two 35mm prints of the finished film will be delivered to your home screening room. And when you see your picture, whether it's an *Eraserhead*-influenced bris or a *Raging Bull*–esque first T-ball game, we guarantee it will be more absorbing than the actual event. Director reserves the right to cast all nonprincipal roles, has script approval and final cut. No producer credit for purchaser. ***Cinéma du Jour Grand: $60 million.***

You've invested in new clubs, years of lessons, a private driving range, even a caddy with dubious scorekeeping skills—all in a single-minded attempt to shave strokes off your game. Still, a day on the links frustrates you, reduces you to a club-twisting, pro-firing, range-torching caddy-beater. Well, we think it's time you showed your foursome, your country club, the sport, who's boss. And the Titleist Uno lets you do just that. The Uno is the last word in golf technology as well as the last investment you ever need make in the game. Because the Titleist Uno lowers your score till it can be lowered no more. Inside this regulation ball is a high-energy, high-ion plasma core for distance far beyond your power; a gyroscopic stabilizer for true flight that belies your flawed mechanics; an on-board, flag-seeking laser sight; and an electromagnetic impulse oscillator that locks onto and is drawn not to the pin or cup (illegal) but to the hole or void (unruled on). The Titleist Uno delivers an ace every hole! An eighteen every round! Meaning if you don't win, somebody's cheating. *Titleist Uno (box of 1): $99,999.*

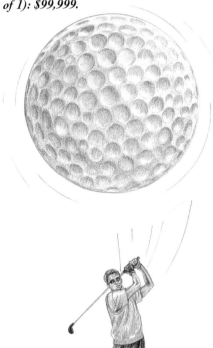

PixNix

To paraphrase Mark Twain: Everybody complains about the paparazzi, but no one does anything about them. We feel certain, then, that the celebrated Mr. Twain would be surprised as well as mightily pleased by the arrival of the PixNix, the first and only reliable foiler of photo obtruders. The PixNix is a pocketsize electronic godsend for the perpetually press oppressed, a device that mitigates fame while leaving fortune intact. It does all this by creating a powerful, impenetrable, proprietary photon dispersion field in the immediate vicinity of its bearer. Now, when a picture is snapped, all people, pets, and things within the "safe zone" are distorted, blurred, rendered unrecognizable and, therefore, unmarketable. You can let the 'razzi click, because your visage simply won't stick. The perfect gift for any object of curiosity, scrutiny, or awestruck wonder on your list. The PixNix stops shutterbugs dead. Effective against all digital, magnetic, and film media/formats. Approximate coverage area: 6-foot radius. Should not be used near children or explosives. ***PixNix: $500,000.***

Is it the negative influence of the paid, lowerclass employees who raise your children? Or is it the kids' innate curiosity regarding boundaries—curiosity indicative of the daring spirit and dynamic intellect they've inherited? Maybe it's their need to actually *feel something*? It's hard to say. But all too often, from Leopold and Loeb to Patty Hearst, William Kennedy Smith to Al Gore III, children of privilege run into trouble with the law. Real, blue-collar trouble. That's why ScionQuest Adventures created Crime Spree Camp. Open to children from 6 through 20, Crime Spree Camp lets your children run rampant, indulging their every criminal tendency in the safety of a closed, controlled environment (actual town to be terrorized TBD). All with no criminal or civil charges, no consequences, no attorneys. From robbery to rape, arson to X dealing, at Crime Spree Camp, anything—and everything—goes. It's the perfect and unprosecutable way to get it out of their systems and, in the process, set your li'l sociopaths on the right path. 30-, 60- and 90-day camps available. Includes 5-star accommodations and all meals. *Crime Spree Camp (per 30-day period): Ringleader Class (unlimited felonies), $20 million/child. Accomplice Class (choice of three felonies, unlimited misdemeanors), $12 million/child.*

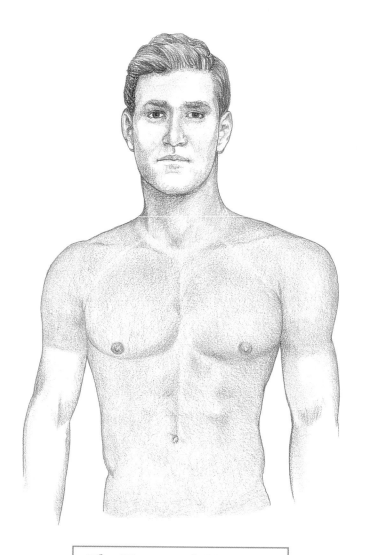

The Emperor's New Tee

This outstanding top-of-the line tee shirt is the next best thing to nothing next to your skin. Made of 100% diaphanous Tibetan spider silk spun in the almost airless air of the Himalayan peaks, you'll find it difficult if not impossible to see … unless you're the kind of man who knows what to look for. The Emperor's New Tee weighs in at less than .01 grams and is perfect for those occasions when you can't decide between going bare-chested and throwing on the least possible covering. Tailored in Italy by Ermenegildo Zegna's cooler, older brother, Ugo. Tee should be returned to manufacturer for laundering. *The Emperor's New Tee (specify Invisible Umber, Imperceptible Sage, or Bright Clear): $1,599.99. Laundering (including overnight return delivery): $399.99.*

Kevlar Threads

Protests and sit-ins are taking place on college campuses everywhere, from New Haven to Cambridge, Princeton to Hanover. And even though the tragedy of Kent State took place at a state university somewhere in the lawless non-East, who knows where or when violence may erupt again? Fortunately, Kevlar Threads will keep your child safe from harm during any peace-incited violence. These clothes ("threads," in the vernacular of the young) are styled to look like today's latest (non)fashions—bell-bottom jeans, tie-dyed and batiked tee-shirts, furry vests, dashikis, ponchos, even headbands—but are made of 100% Kevlar. What's Kevlar? Scheduled to be introduced to police departments in vest form next year, Kevlar is a revolutionary lightweight synthetic—and *bulletproof*—fiber developed and manufactured by DuPont. Send your teenager off to school dressed in these "hippie" garments, knowing he or she is impervious to stray or even directed gunfire. It's peace of mind for parents of peaceniks. Set includes five pairs of pants, ten tops, ten accessories. ***Kevlar Threads: $250,000.***

It's generally held that you can't be too rich or too thin. And a cursory glance at your portfolio, not to mention your inclusion on our mailing list, makes a good case for the former. As for the latter, well, let's just say that despite spas, trainers, Atkins, South Beach, liposuction, Spandex, ex-lax, and ipecac, there's still some trophy whore or mummified old moneybags at the club who's a few pounds lighter than you. No more. Slightening is a patented surgical process that removes, in whole or in part, every extraneous and superfluous gland, organ, appendage, tissue, and fluid in your body. Reducing your total post-op weight by as much as 10 to 15 pounds. With no appreciable drop in body functions. Not enough? Replace dense, heavy bone with strong, lightweight, custom-cast titanium for even further weight savings. Only Slightening promises to make you far less than you ever dreamed. *Slightening: between $18 and $20 million. Add titanium bone replacement for approximately $25 million. (Price and results vary by the number of surgeries required and available superfluous body components.)*

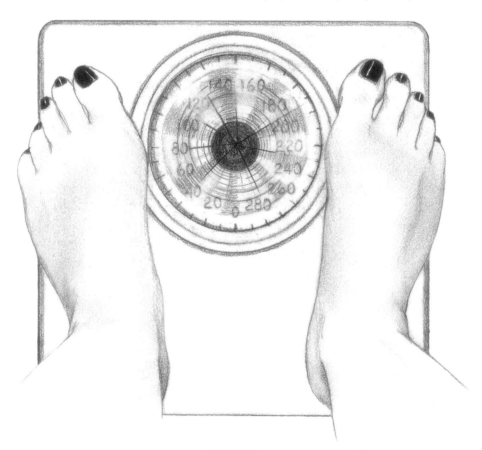

TrumpAway Spray

It never fails. You're having a quiet dinner with friends at a favorite midtown bistro—a bistro whose expense, exclusivity, and *hush-hush* location guarantees a certain clientele and atmosphere. You order a coelacanth steak, *truffles frites*, and a vintage bottle of wine that costs more than a month stay at the Betty Ford Center. Then just as your meal arrives, the unthinkable, the untenable, the unbearable happens: Donald Trump bursts through the door. Immediately, brass and brazenness fills the room. The atmosphere turns fetid. Your appetite, along with your will to live, evaporates. Well, no more. TrumpAway Spray keeps the Donald at bay … up to 100 feet away. Just spray this potent repellent around the perimeter of the area you wish to protect, and you've put up a scent barrier the blow-dried blowhard simply can't penetrate. For up to 6 full and blessed hours. Scientifically formulated from sources as diverse as the pheromones of sincere people, sweat of the poor man's brow, tears shed by women over 40, oil of bankruptcy lawyer, hairspray solvent, and liquid dignity. ***TrumpAway Spray (4-ounce spray bottle; approximately 8 uses): $160,000.***

Porch-o-Rama

There's something quintessentially American about the front porch. From coast to coast, the front porch is our most egalitarian display of neighborliness. An eloquent expression of sociability, tradition, and shared values. Two problems though: (1) Your secluded estate isolates you from any neighbors. (2) You like it that way. Two problems solved: Porch-o-Rama. Porch-o-Rama delivers the front porch experience without exposing you to the humanity commonly associated with thriving communities. It works like this: First, our skilled environmental architects add an absolutely archetypal porch to the front of your existing home. Next, around your new porch we construct and install a 180° HD projection Surround Screen and Surround Sound system. Playing on-screen, 24/7, will be a live closed-circuit broadcast of the homespun sights and sounds of one of this country's most active, outgoing—and distant!—heartland communities. Suddenly, life is all around you, but, just as importantly, not touching you. So go ahead: Wave hello and call to passersby. Enjoy the children playing "in the yard across the street." Watch the neighborhood dogs frolic, with no fear of them soiling your lawn. "Publicly" imbibe in your rarest of brandies without ever having to share. It's the best of both worlds: All the advantages of yours, none of the downsides of theirs. ***Porch-o-Rama: $499 million.***

We've all seen the news stories. "Heiress Charged With Drunk Driving." "Superstar Enters Rehab." "Powerful Pundit Busted for Prescription Drug Fraud." "Superstar Enters Rehab. Again." These are cautionary tales, tales that warn us: Don't get caught attempting to relieve the terrible pressures of an incomprehensibly demanding life. And with Anēbria, you won't. Because Anēbria is a revolutionary recreational drug formulated to provide an undetectable, nonaddictive feeling of extreme euphoria with absolutely no loss of judgment, physical dexterity, or bladder control. With no side effects. None. It's like doing a shovelful of righteous blow minus the intense craving and perforated nasal septum. This is the substance all America's been waiting to abuse! And that wait will continue. Because the FDA, fearing the collapse of the alcohol and narcotics industries, will not allow Anēbria to go to market. Now, however, in an exclusive arrangement with the watchdog agency, Serfitt & Cloye is making this wonder/ful drug legally available to one lucky family ("family" defined as two parents and up to seven dependents). Feel the bliss. Without the bad press. Dosage varies by body weight and strength of will. *Anēbria (specify snortable, shootable, freebase-able or easy-to-swallow gel caplet form): $500,000 minimum order (approximately one person's one-year supply).*

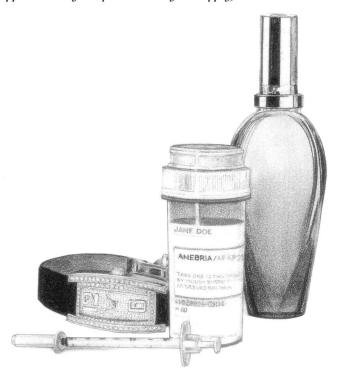

Frank Gehry Recreational Vehicle

Road trips are transformed into poststructuralist sojourns in überarchitect Frank Gehry's stunning interpretation of the RV. This astonishing motor home is Gehry's first foray into private wheeled-dwelling architecture, and he has, naturally, produced a true *tour*(ing vehicle) *de force*. With every oblique surface, every idiosyncratic angle, every nihilistic nuance a statement as well as an illumination. Clad in a brushed nickel skin, the exterior's eccentric appurtenances and akimbo angularity defy all expectations. Inside, the irregular room shapes and metacontemporary multitiered floor plan demonstrate the aesthetics of spatial disorientation. The vehicle's unconventional-yet-apposite appointments include a climbing wall, sushi bar, cutting garden, and full basement. ***Frank Gehry Recreational Vehicle: $15 million. (Vehicle not designed to fit under conventional overpasses; roll-over may occur on turns of fewer than 120° at speeds in excess of 25 miles per hour; sushi chef and fresh fish not included.)***

1928

Prescription Skyscraper

It hardly seems right: You're master of all you survey, yet you need the panty-waist's accessory—eyeglasses—to survey it. Stand at any window in our Prescription Skyscraper, however, and you can gaze over the farthest reaches of your empire unencumbered by onerous, unattractive corrective eyewear. Because every window of this soaring, 55-story Cass Gilbert–designed structure has been ground to your prescription. Now it's others—unbespectacled subordinates and nameless tenants—who will peer off into the hazy, indistinct outside world from their desks. All interior glass panes—in doors, separating offices, et cetera—are similarly vision corrective. You may never wear glasses at the office again! Make this your empire's HQ. And be a man of vision. Again.

Prescription Skyscraper (built in the metropolis of your choice, on your deeded lot): $28 million. (Ask about our companion Prescription Manor for home use.)

Garbage Defense System

Your garbage tells a story. A story that's nobody's business. Trouble is, once your refuse is placed at the curb, it's in the public domain. Free for the taking. And scrutinizing. And analyzing. Next thing you know, you're being indicted or humiliated or both. That's why it's so important to dispose of your waste wisely. Self-protectively. The Garbage Defense System is your foolproof firewall against garbage pickers, refuse perusers, and trash hackers. Simply insert your garbage, by the piece or the pile, into the (supplied) appropriate-size puncture-, rip-, and tamper-proof carbon-fiber trash bags, then place the bag into one of the GDS pneumatic tube openings conveniently wall-mounted throughout your home. In a flash, your garbage is whisked away to an exclusive private underground garbage dump located deep beneath your city's public above-ground garbage dump. Big enough, deep enough, secure enough to hold all the secret documents, Hot Pockets wrappers, purgatives, escort service receipts, and leather adult diapers you can throw at it. *Garbage Defense System (includes a starter set of variably sized bags, up to 10 pneumatic openings throughout your house, and installation of underground home-to-dump pneumatic conduit): $20 million.*

Great affluence and lofty social standing can only unlevel the playing field so much for children. To tip it in their direction conclusively—to ensure one's scion enjoys all that life has to offer—means giving him or her all the educational opportunities obtainable. And Fetus University delivers the first of those opportunities before baby's even delivered. FU has assembled a distinguished full-time faculty of pioneering prenatal PhDs to instruct your child in utero over a 2-semester program that will coincide with the second and third trimesters. Through the use of special intravaginal projectors and abdominally mounted subcutaneous speakers (designed by BabyBose, a division of Bose Corporation), professors will create a visually stimulating, acoustically perfect amniotic learning environment. The umbilically bound student will be exposed to music, art, natural history, vocabulary and reading, basic math, and lacrosse. To simulate the classroom experience as closely as possible, lectures and video presentations will be live rather than recorded, with the school day lasting a total of 6 hours. Approximately 2 hours of homework will be assigned per day. *Fetus University (includes all faculty, travel to the mother's locale, lodging allowances, and audio/visual equipment): $650,000.*

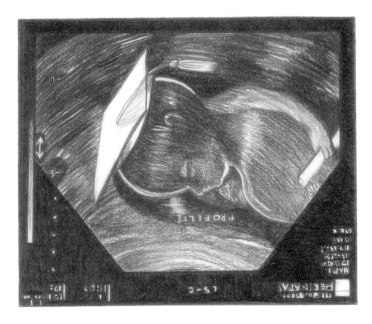

Benard Gjerrie Ice Cream

On 1,000 acres of verdant pasture outside Bern, Switzerland, lives Gisele, a two-year-old dairy cow. Gisele has the entire farm to herself, grazing on tender shoots and clover during warmer months, crunching organic grains and legumes in the barn when the temperature turns cold. She receives the finest veterinary care available, but has never been given a single cc of vaccines, antibiotics, or hormones. Her owner, Benard Gjerrie, brushes and massages his lone cow nightly in the soft orange glow of aromatherapy candles. As one might imagine, Gisele is not merely contented, she is fulfilled. What one can't imagine is the impact this healthful, stress-free lifestyle has on her milk. A mere sip of this molten white gold saturates one's very soul in ecstasy and butterfat, inspiring joyful psalms to bovine achievement. But a sip will have to do. Because Gisele's entire annual output is already spoken for: It will become ice cream. Benard Gjerrie makes the frozen confection right on his farm, adding only all natural, small-batch, organic ingredients to Gisele's über-uddercraft. With nary an additive, emulsifier or chemical. Production is on-demand and limited to 2,000 gallons. *Benard Gjerrie Vanilla (per gallon): $500. Benard Gjerrie Chocolate (per gallon): $600. Additional flavors: Call for a quote. (Shipping from Switzerland extra.)*

Matriarch Eau de Parfum

To anyone who's perused the myriad popular scents available at perfume counters today, the tawdry bottles bearing the names of film stars and celebutantes, we pose this question: Why smell like a whore when you can smell like a grande dame? Matriarch, the latest fragrance by Parisian *parfumeur* Claude Haupert, can imbue even the *nouveau*-est *riche* with the unequivocal, unmistakable air of the *ancien régime*. Swathe the tartiest upstart in the heady bouquet of heritage, respectability, dignity, grace, and disdain. The scent delicately mingles such *notes aromatiques* as camphor, cedar, lavender, honey, menthol, naphtha, face powder, buffered aspirin, musk, and sherry, then underscores them with leathery notes of royal equestrian saddles and Hyannisport antique den chairs. Matriarch exudes a mature prosperity that eclipses—even crushes—youthful sensuality. This, then, is the scent of a woman … of privilege. Packaged in a 24-karat white-gold 1.6-ounce vial with a 5-carat diamond stopper. *Matriarch Eau de Parfum: $100,000.*

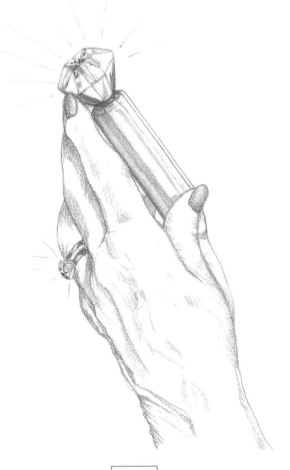

New Yankee Kindling

There is, perhaps, no more respected craftsman in America than Norm Abram, host of and master carpenter on the PBS series *The New Yankee Workshop*. By the same token, there's probably also no more discouraging, more galling craftsman than the selfsame Mr. Abram. For nearly twenty years, his aptitude, perfection, freedom from tool-related injury, and dearth of profanity during even the most complex project has rubbed the noses of myriad furniture builders and woodworking hobbyists in an unattainable ideal. But you can turn the solid mahogany, hinge-top Federal-style tables on this bearded virtuoso. With New Yankee Kindling. We've procured every piece of furniture, every outdoor project, every decorative *objet* (including prototypes)—nearly 700 in all—to ever come out of the Workshop, with the express intent of reducing every last stick of it into high-grade, kiln-dried kindling for your fireplace. This is the aggrieved woodworker's singular opportunity to settle the score for countless hours of leisure-time frustration and inadequacy. Can Norm build better furniture than you? Undoubtedly. But he damn sure can't build a better fire. *New Yankee Kindling: $2 million (pre-splintered by Serfitt & Cloye, shipped anywhere in the continental U.S.); $3 million (pieces are shipped unsplintered and accompanied by Norm who watches you destroy them); $3.5 million (as above but Norm conducts a personal two-day hands-on seminar, demonstrating the best tools and methods for smashing furniture).*

If you can make people laugh, it's a gift. If you can make people laugh with a gift, it must be one of our super-nice-but-super-sized novelty items. There's the enormous watch, made from one of Big Ben's four clocks, with the works housed in a stainless steel watch back and finished off with a strapping genuine alligator band. Or how about our wacky oversized cushion-cut 1000-carat emerald? Far too big for a pendant, altogether too small for an ottoman, but just right for hilarity. For your smoking friends, we have the jumbo novelty Montecristo cigar, Cuban-made to be sure, but—holy cow!—running the full length of Cuba as well. Finally, big-time wildlife fans will love our big-time teddy bear stitched together from over 30 polar bear skins and plushly stuffed with another 400! One thing to keep in mind though: There may be price tags on these items, but the laughs are priceless. ***Big Ben Watch: $150 million. Oversize Emerald: $55 million. Jumbo Montecristo: $1.5 million. Super-Duper Teddy Bear: $4.5 million.***

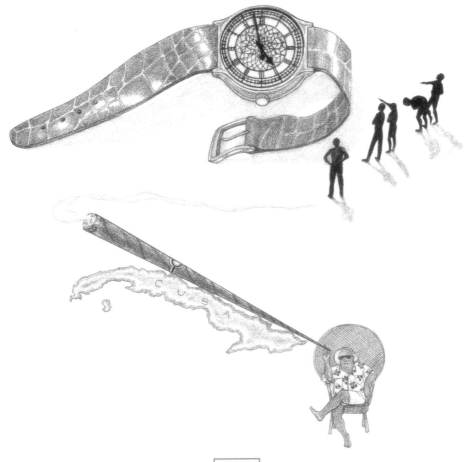

Unlisted Number License Plate

There was a time, long, long ago, when vanity plates *said* something. Something about *you*. Your identity. And your readiness to pay a little extra for freedom of expression. Then came the arrivistes. The imitators. And suddenly, your uniquely you "ITSME" plate turned up in countless unclever variations, like "ITSMEII" and "ITSME3" and "ITSME97." Maybe you even spotted an identical, mocking "ITSME" plate from a neighboring state. Gadzooks, is it any wonder there's so much road rage? How fortuitous, then, that the opportunity to express your unambiguous individuality through the medium of your vehicle's tags is back. In spades. And in perpetuity. With the Unlisted Number License Plate. This tag, a simple, striking color field, has no state affiliation, no letters, no numbers, no dates, and it's registered in all 50 states—so copies, in whole or in part, in-state or out, are impossible. And it never has to be renewed. Order now. Just one plate in each primary color is available. ***Unlisted Number License Plate: $899,000, plus $6.25 unwaivable processing fee.***

SubZero AbsoluteZero Freezer

Half measures aren't your style. So when you put something in the kitchen freezer, you don't want it to merely be frozen, you want it to be thoroughly and completely frozen—that is, frozen to the maximum extent achievable according to the laws of physics, not the lax conventions of home refrigeration. And that maximum is not zero degrees Fahrenheit. Or even zero degrees Celsius. It's zero degrees Kelvin—absolute zero (that's -459.67° Fahrenheit; -273.15° Celsius, respectively). The SubZero AbsoluteZero Freezer delivers this lowest of temps with the highest of styles. Available in a variety of noble metals with brushed finishes, this 30-square-foot-capacity appliance can flash freeze any item or substance placed in its frosty maw: pizza or protons, ice cream or inert gases, Lean Cuisine or cryogenic experiments. Best of all, you get the peace of mind that comes with knowing any potentially damaging or degrading subatomic motion in your frozen matter (or antimatter!) is halted dead in its tracks. The Tater Tots you put in today won't just be good next week, they'll be good next geological era. Mmm-mmm. The SubZero AbsoluteZero Freezer. Elevating home freezing to a science. Shipped with one pair of ergonomic 5-foot tongs for item insertion/removal. *SubZero Absolute Zero Freezer: $159 million.*

Vins de Limo

Having a glass of wine in the back of your limousine can be quite an adventure. Quick stops, sudden maneuvers, potholes, and the like can all add up to spills. Leaving you stained or, worse, robbing you of a last taste of an extraordinary vintage. Which is what makes Vins de Limo such a remarkable find. Vins de Limo are the fine wines oenologists most enjoy, but with an additional 22% viscosity, a viscosity that reduces sloshing and spilling by 60% and 75%, respectively. Each bottle is derived (by a proprietary process overseen by France's Institut National des Appellations d'Origine) from the most acclaimed chateaux, the most desired and rarest vintages. Serfitt & Cloye unconditionally guarantees the taste of Vins de Limo to be absolutely indistinguishable from the thin, traditional wines from which they're produced—whether a 1978 Montrachet or a 1787 Chateau d'Yquem. Never spill another drop of your precious spirits, or fire another chauffer because you have. ***Vins de Limo (per case): From $299,000 to $1 million.***

"Peace" of Mind Coasters

What do Theodore Roosevelt, Martin Luther King, and Lech Walesa have in common? All three are wonderful at safeguarding furniture from the unsightly water rings drippy drink glasses can leave. Of course, we're not talking about the great men themselves; we're talking about their respective Nobel Peace Prize medals, which we've elegantly transformed into handsome, hard-wearing coasters. But in addition to those already mentioned, we've also obtained the Peace Prizes of 22 of the most popular Laureates, for a grand total of 25 coasters. Imagine the prestige of placing a G&T on Nelson Mandela. Or the cosmic symbolism of Elie Wiesel protecting against spilled schnapps. Or the righteousness of setting only empty glasses on Mother Teresa. Or the satisfaction of never using Jimmy Carter. Keep in mind, these are not replicas, but the actual medals awarded to the Laureates. Each is a conversation piece forged in gold. And worth its weight in gold for the protection it provides fine furniture. Dishwasher safe. Sold (as they were purchased) under a strict "no questions asked" policy. ***Nobel Peace Prize coasters (set of 25): $6.25 million.***

Self-Cleaning Décor

First, there's the language problem. Not to mention their sad, pitiful eyes. Then there's the tiresome prospect of an untimely INS raid. Of course, looming largest is the inevitable suspicion and/or reality of thievery. Alas, it would seem the many downsides to hiring domestic cleaning help far outweigh the upside. Fortunately, your homes can now be spic and span without a spi … that is, a Spanish-speaking staff. Our ingenious self-cleaning décor eliminates the need for minority-performed dusting, wiping, vacuuming, or cleaning of any kind. With this service, each piece of hard-surfaced furniture, solid flooring, and work of art in your home will receive and hold a low-level antielectrostatic charge, just enough to repel airborne particulates, so they never land. In a delectable bit of synergy, upholstered furniture, rugs, and other soft surfaces will be embedded with genetically engineered microbes that actually "eat" (absorb) the skin cells, plant pollen, and other components of common household dust; drips and spills get gobbled up, too. Your house stays clean, you don't get cleaned out by outsiders. *Self-Cleaning Décor (one home, up to 20,000 square feet): $3.3 million.*

Position and privilege make military service an unnecessary, unthinkable career option for your child. But just because he won't be making the ultimate sacrifice for his country doesn't mean he should be denied the thrill of command, the charge of supersonic flight, the ecstasy of unleashing unimaginable force. And as captain of the USS *Happy Birthday*, he won't. This is your chance to throw your scion the ultimate birthday bash. Aboard the biggest tub in all the seven seas. It starts when your child and up to 12 guests (along with nanny or parent) are flown by the Blue Angels to a fully armed and operational aircraft carrier (the USS *Abraham Lincoln*, location TBD). Upon deplaning, your son (or other-gendered child) will be greeted by the unfurling of a large congratulatory banner ("It's your Birthday! Mission Accomplished!"), be presented with a rear admiral's hat, and take the ship's helm as its highest-ranking officer. As ship's commander, he'll set course, steer, bark orders, bust crewmembers in rank, even issue binding Section 8s. As the sun sets, it's fireworks time, and your li'l admiral remains largest and in chargest, personally firing six RIM-7P NATO Sea Sparrow "heir-to-air" missiles programmed to gloriously, deafeningly detonate directly overhead. After birthday cake and ice cream in the officers' mess, it's back in the F/A-18's cockpit for the ride home. This is a high-flyin', boat-floatin' 12-hour celebratory tour of duty your child will never forget. Or have to repeat. ***USS* Happy Birthday: *$19.25 million (includes $10 million contribution to the Republican National Committee.)***

Personal Transplant Concierge

Waiting in line for coffee is hell. Waiting in line for tickets is hell. Even waiting for the assistant you sent to wait in line for your coffee or tickets is hell. So imagine the frustration and aggravation of waiting, waiting, waiting on a long, long list in order to get the vital internal organ you need to survive. Gadzooks! Fortunately, your Personal Transplant Concierge eliminates that possibility. Through this health professional's worldwide network of accomplished organ procurement operatives, and his extensive knowledge of where life is cheapest—not to mention his timely, generous, and *sub-rosa* fiduciary enticements to interested parties— your next liver, kidney, lung, heart (you name it) will practically be in the OR before you are. But don't take our word for it. The Concierge comes with this guarantee: Your replacement organ—fresh, operational, and of matching blood type—will be delivered within 30 hours, or it's free. But hurry. The PTC's client list is limited to three. Meaning that, in this instance, the only thing to come to those who wait is waiting to die. ***Personal Transplant Concierge: $100 million. (Lifetime retainer, good for up to five organs. Surgery, hospital stay, and post-operative medications not included.)***

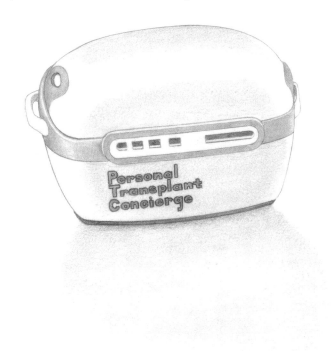

1915

Royal Court Cure

Do you or does someone you love suffer from chilblains? Ague? Brain fever? Influenza? Hemophilia? Rheumatism? Small pox? Large pox? Melancholia? Shell shock? Pancreatic malaise? Brisbane's disquiet? Hypochondriachal hysteria? No matter. You'll soon suffer no more. By exclusive arrangement with the Tsar and Tsarina of Russia, you (or your designate) shall be granted an audience with the healer and mystic Grigori Rasputin, whereupon he shall immediately exorcize any ailment(s) or symptom(s) that currently afflict you. As Tsar Nicholas II says, "When it comes to restoring your health, there's no disputin' Rasputin." ***Royal Court Cure: $500,000. (Includes first-class travel arrangements and accommodations; not responsible for carnal importuning.)***

Oracular Bubble Wrap

For years, popping bubble wrap has been a simple, undirected pleasure enjoyed by people of all ages and incomes. No more. Oracular Bubble Wrap elevates the noisy, mindless activity of Everyman to the level of mystical sacrament for the receptive cognoscenti. With OBW, each poppable plastic compartment on every jumbo roll is filled with ethylene gas, a substance that, when inhaled by deep-breathing bubble-bursters, will induce euphoria. But this isn't just any ethylene gas. Ours is scrupulously collected from the steep, deep limestone fissures of Mount Parnassus in central Greece, the very same mountain where the Oracle of Delphi delivered the prophecies of the Gods and is the very same ethylene gas, archeological pharmacologists deduce, that induced her soothsaying trances. This, then, is a win-win-win: the gratification of bubble-wrap popping; mellow euphoria; and visions of the future. Never has knowing when to buy or sell stocks, how to manipulate a market, or whom to marry or disinherit been so fun, so easy, so clear, so delightfully noisy. Practically pays for itself. *Oracular Bubble Wrap (3-foot x 100-foot roll): $600,000.*

ORDERING

1. Select the item(s) you wish to order.

2. Tell your assistant.

3. Everything will be taken care of.

METHODS OF PAYMENT

Serfitt & Cloye accepts
American Express Plutonium Card,
cash transfers from foreign banks,
and gold bullion.

Humborghini

Sacrifice and compromise are two sides of the same miserable, devalued coin. A coin the Humborghini is doing its best to remove from circulation. Be warned, however: This groundbreaking, groundshaking, all-terrain armored racing coupe is neither for the faint nor the bleeding of heart. The sole car ever to be produced jointly by AM General and Automobili Lamborghini, the Humborghini is a suave and sturdy synthesis of Humvee's finest military multipurpose tactical vehicle and Lamborghini's wind-slicing high-performance supercar. Powered by a V-24 1,500-horsepower engine (.25 miles per gallon highway, -.25 miles per gallon city), this sleek beast has the power to haul a train car or, should one prefer, some serious ass. With a top speed of 235 miles per hour on level blacktop, 215 miles per hour on the steepest, craggiest snowcap. Its Adaptiflex suspension can easily conquer hill and dale, smooth out the roughest backcountry washboard, or glide like butter on an unspoiled private drive. And because it's fully up-armored and fitted with bulletproof glass, it's as safe as it is swift, able to withstand machine-gun fire, IED blasts, and the occasional grocery cart alike. The Humborghini is the ideal vehicle to take one to the ends of the earth or, for that matter, to get one through End Times. Sacrifice and compromise? This is the automobile to flatten 'em dead. ***Humborghini: $1.7 million.***

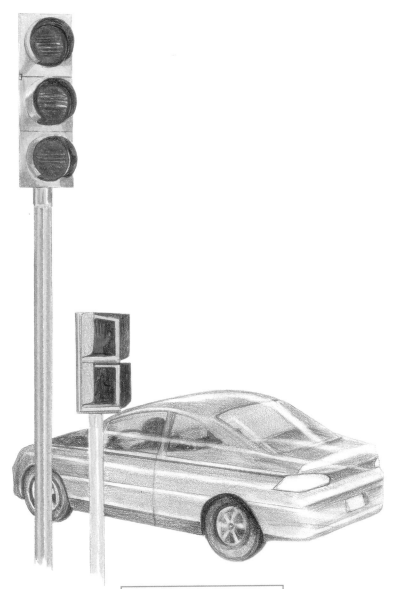

Green Means Go

Still stopping at red lights with the rest of motoring's losers? You needn't. Green Means Go is a sleek dashboard-mounted device that "reads" the color of the upcoming traffic signal and, when it sees red, emits a microwave beam to the signal control box; the offending light automatically changes to green just as you get there. Every road, every lane, every hour of every of day, is a nonstop express. Best of all, there's only one. That way you never have to worry that some other well-heeled motorist is going to change the light on *you*. *Green Means Go: $750,000.*

SteadiYacht

It seems no matter how long one's yacht is, it's still subject to the swaying and swelling of the sea. All well and good for those who like their ship's rails crowded with guests heaving up caviar and Cristal. For everyone else, there's SteadiYacht, just launched by Oceanada, the renowned Portuguese shipbuilder. On the surface, SteadiYacht looks like any other 450-foot, high-speed, luxury watercraft. But on closer inspection one finds something else: It's actually a yacht within a yacht. And this marvel of marine engineering effectively eliminates all heave, pitch, and roll. It works like this: The inner vessel's hull is completely isolated from the outer by a 12-foot cushion of high-viscosity, low-friction, polyhydrogenated lubricant, and suspended by a freely pivoting isoelastic armature interfacing with a patented system of computer-assisted gyroscopic counterweights capable of achieving a hydrostability score of .063 units of maritime flux. But for all the esoteric sophistication and opaque intricacies, SteadiYacht's triumph is as plain as the first nose on a second wife's face: Standing topside in 20-foot swells, one can look at the horizon with no discernable horizontal or vertical motion. Includes helipad/helicopter, two 40-foot sport-fishing boats, wine cellar, fish hatchery, organic garden and more. *SteadiYacht: $375 million. (SteadiCrew sold separately.)*

Executive Branch Privilege

There's no truer patriot, no greater visionary, no more powerful man in all America than Vice-President Dick Cheney. So it is with pride that Serfitt & Cloye now offers one lucky neocon consumer the opportunity not only to get to know the Commander in Chief's Commander in Chief, but to receive from him a personal, limited-edition souvenir: facial birdshot-scarring. The arrangement: In mid-February, 2006, you'll fly via Air Force Two to an undisclosed south Texas ranch for an intimate meet-and-greet with the Veep. On two consecutive mornings, the Vice-President, you, and a select hunting party will travel by armored Humvee cortège to a plushly appointed blind where you'll shoot small birds thrown into your line of fire by avian launch specialists. Late the second day, after cocktail hour, you'll undergo anesthetization from the neck up and, once you're fully numb, Mr. Cheney will take up his shotgun and shoot you in the face. You'll feel no pain; medical attention will be immediate; air MEDEVAC to your private hospital suite is included. Once the bandages come off, you'll be sporting a completely permanent, totally unignorable, thoroughly envy-eliciting mark of distinction. A "veep-sake" you'll thank him for (required). Don't miss out. This is a priceless story absolutely no one will be able to top: spending "face (changing) time" with your pal, "The Dick." ***Executive Branch Privilege: $5 million.***

Towhead Club Tie

Gifting Dad with a tie for Christmas doesn't show much imagination. Unless, of course, you're giving the Towhead Club Tie. With this dashing bit of haberdashery, you're sure to quickly and curry-lessly gain Dad's favor. It's made of 100% Scandinavian cashmere, a neonatural fiber made from the feather-soft fleece atop the heads of the blondest, palest newborns in Sweden's blondest, palest town, Tjåguoristugan. The fleece is gathered by mothers who gently comb their babies' hair every day for the first week of their lives. Each precious, downy strand relinquished by pate to the comb is collected, spun into yarn, and woven with peerless Nordic nitpickery on foot-treadle floor looms. The raw, unbleached, ultra-supple textile is then dyed, using vibrant organic pigments derived from rare heirloom fruits, vegetables, and flowers grown in the sun-drenched soil of the Orinoco basin by Los Hermanos de Abono Caballo, a reclusive order of horticulturist defrocked priests. The tie's distinctive colors and copyrighted striped pattern are exclusive to and used by permission of Yale University's League of Patrimony, the super-secret society of supra-societal crème that not only predates the far more overt Order of Skull and Bones, but is, to this day, annually fellated by its lesser brethren. Truly, this is an accessory for the necks of the Gods. Like Dad. *Towhead Club Tie: $9,999.*

Know someone who simply has to be the smartest person in the room? Let fMRIQ make sure he or she is. Quantifiably. fMRIQ invisibly transforms an entire room (your choice of home living room or office conference room) into a Cedars-Sinai-quality functional magnetic resonant imaging (fMRI) machine, taking high-technology, high-speed, high-resolution brain scans of everyone contained within its four walls. The scans capture concrete information like brain volume and mass as well as more fluid intracranial data like blood flow and brain wave activity (EEG). These readings and measurements are streamed in real time to an onsite Cray supercomputer, then analyzed and interpreted using proprietary software. The resulting IQ assessment of each scanned person is then relayed wirelessly to a companion Blackberry device held by the "interested party." Within one minute of entering the fMRIQ diagnostic environment, the smartest person in the room will know precisely who the smartest person in the room is and, should it not be him or her, who has to go to make things right. *fMRIQ: $33 million.*

Erection Insurance

Male genitalia is notoriously erratic, susceptible to influences as serious as prostate surgery, and as frivolous as the wrong brand of whipped topping. For the vast majority of victims, regardless of which side of the penis you're on, erection failure is frustrating, utterly unacceptable. And while erectile dysfunction may frequently respond to familiar remedies like vulgar encouragement or prescription drugs, the sad fact is, neither of these solutions gets at the heart of the matter: Someone must pay—for the embarrassment, the inconvenience, the distress, the ungratification. And we've found someone who will pay: Lloyd's of London. Through exclusive arrangement with the legendary British insurer, Serfitt & Cloye is honored to offer one randy couple (regardless of marital status or sexual orientation) a most fitting fiscal response to a deleterious genitalogical failure. The insured must be in excellent health (doctor's examination required) and have no history of "wood fatigue" (a complete list of former relationships required). *Erection Insurance: $12 million. (Benefit is $1 million per dysfunction, pending inspection by claims adjuster; claims may affect future premiums. Sorry, polygamists and persons dating Ann Coulter are ineligible for coverage.)*

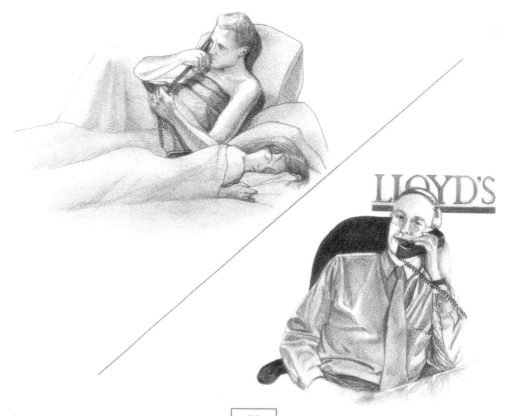

Belgian Bonsai Dark Chocolate

The discipline of the East meets the indulgence of the West in this grand confectionary convergence. Since 1975, on a lush and sweltering hectare in southern Indonesia, over one thousand potted bonsai cacao trees have been patiently cultivated by Japanese horticultural sensei. After 32 years of restricted growth and meticulous manipulation, the miniature forest has at last produced its first equally miniature fruit (each bonsai cacao pod and its beans are 1/75 normal size); the entire harvest could be held in a single attaché case. As growers had hoped, the bonsai beans yielded a dizzyingly concentrated, staggeringly dense and intense chocolateness, what those in the confection sciences began to describe as "a collapsed star of cocoa." This savory treasure was subsequently hand-carried to Brugge, Belgium, and the kitchens of Kavittiez, the original Royal Chocolatiers to King Leopold I. There, micro-beans, pure pre-Castro archival Cuban cane sugar, and nearly 180 years of chocolate expertise and artistry came together to create precisely 5.3 pounds of 82.5% cocoa rapture. For the late-stage chocoholic on your list. *Belgian Bonsai Dark Chocolate (5.3-pound box, 100 pieces): $150,000.*

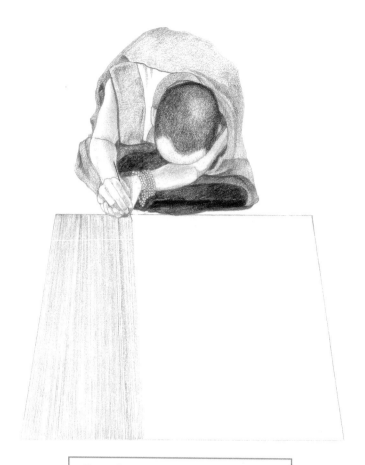

Semiprecious Seersucker

Seersucker is a timeless fashion classic, like bowties and saddle shoes. Among certain circles in certain places under certain circumstances, it's even regarded as the official garb *d'été*. Which is not to say it can't be refreshed or improved. It can. And Semiprecious Seersucker does just that, putting a differentiating new wrinkle in the already wrinkled. What sets our seersucker apart are two things: the crisp artistry of its stripes; and the vibrancy, consistency, and harmony of its colors. The former is realized not by machine dyeing but through the fastidious precision of a master Tibetan calligrapher carefully applying each narrow vertical stripe to the cotton fabric, using a virgin 102-hair sable brush for each new stripe. As for its colors, the profound, luminous white and deliciously vivid blue are achieved by using dyes imbued with, respectively, finely crushed conch pearls and pulverized lapis lazuli (ultramarine). It's a simply spectacular addition to your wardrobe. Even more so should it be partnered with bowtie or saddle shoes. (Only a quarter-bolt of Semiprecious Seersucker will be produced, but that should provide enough material for multiple outfits, depending on type and size. Shipped directly to your personal tailor.) *Semiprecious Seersucker: $799,000.*

Felis Comis

Who was it that said, "For every cat lover there's a cat that doesn't give a damn"? It hardly matters. Because finally, after nearly 10,000 years of a one-way human-feline relationship, it's not true. Meet Mimi, the one cat who cares. That inter-relates. That gives more than she takes. A sophisticated blend of wild and domesticated cats, Mimi's perfect size, shape, coat, coloration, and markings are the result of over 16 generations of selective feline breeding; her warm, loving, devoted, uncatlike disposition, however, is the result of replacing one critical chromosomal pair with a pair from a Labrador retriever. The result is purrr-fection. Mimi is 1 year old, is guaranteed against coyness and coldness, eschews finickiness, and consistently displays delight in the company of her owner(s). She is trained to come, sit, stay, lie down, fetch, walk on a leash, and accept the right of birds and small mammals to exist. *Felis Comis: $100,000.*

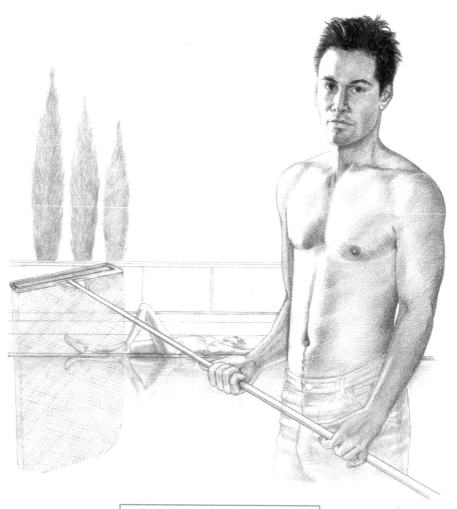

Pool Boy of the Month

Some film actors are all about the craft. Some are all about the paycheck. Our Pool Boy of the Month service delivers twelve of the latter's biggest names to your servant's entrance door on the first day of every month for one full year. Imagine the delight of your children when they discover Keanu Reeves skimming the deep end for leaves. Or the delicious *schadenfreude* of your guests as they send John Travolta to get them towels. Who'll turn up next? Nicholas Cage? Harrison Ford? Ben Stiller? Leave that to us. But rest assured, whoever it is has been fully instructed on the proper performance of their pool-related tasks as well as their proper place in your household, and he'll act the role as well as he can. Guaranteed no television or stage actors. ***Pool Boy of the Month (1-year subscription): $250 million. (Sexual privileges, straight: call for quote. Sexual privileges, gay: call for off-the-record quote.)***

Polo is a game that unites man of means and horse of great expense. The Equestri-Cizer allows players to improve their game and protect their investment by making it possible to train and practice inside. No more riding in the rain or cold, where most mount injuries—not to mention mounted's chapped lips—occur. Essentially, the EquestriCizer is a precision-crafted, Swiss-built treadmill for horse and rider. But its extraordinary features take it well beyond the essential. The flexible tread is covered in BermudaTrue®, an artificial turf so real in look and performance one may be tempted to send a Mexican yard boy out to mow it. The footing/field condition of the "turf" is adjustable, with settings for "Pristine," "Divoted," and "Muddy." Powering the unit is a 5-horsepower, variable-gait drive engine. Built-in Environmental Replicator can be programmed to realistically simulate a range of wind conditions, sun angles, and crowd noise. Plus, should Old Paint prove to be a less than worthy mount, just initiate the Purge Sequence and an integrated Ruger rifle will automatically put the substandard steed down, even calling the nearest pet food company to arrange pickup. *EquestriCizer: $899,000. (Installation extra).*

Ante-Orchestra Seats

Where does an 800-pound theater-loving gorilla sit? Anywhere she wants to.
Which most often means front row center. But is this *really* the best she can do?
After all, couldn't the she-ape (and her he-ape companion) get a closer look and
more immersive theater experience by climbing on stage? Why, yes, they could.
And can. Ante-Orchestra Seats are one astonishing pair of seats placed on stage
for one performance (your choice of date) of every Broadway, Off-Broadway,
and Off-Off-Broadway show currently playing in New York, as well as for all
new productions opening there before December 31, 2009. You'll also have
stage seats for every Radio City Music Hall entertainment extravaganza and
performance, including concerts, the acclaimed Christmas Spectacular, and the
63rd annual Tony Awards. Seats themselves are semi-reclining, upholstered in
buttery lambskin leather with massage mode. *Ante-Orchestra Seats, one pair:*
$12 million. (Intermission refreshments not included.)

We've given the fine old tradition of family game night a fine art twist. Or should we say several twists. First, there's a brain-bending 10,000-piece jigsaw puzzle made from Jackson Pollack's *Untitled* (1948–1949; 45 1/8" x 87 1/8"inches). To create this masterpiece of a puzzle, the canvas was mounted onto a solid sheet of mahogany, laid out in an intricate pattern of interlocking pieces, then meticulously cut by hand with a coping saw. A challenge for even the most expert puzzler! Next, it's a darts match using Jasper Johns's *Target With Four Faces* (1955) mounted on pub-quality corkboard and fitted with a chalkboard for scoring; two sets of three encaustic-strength darts included. Then it's an uproarious game of Twister on a giant mat made from four conjoined "spot" paintings (*Valium 2000*, 2000) by Damien Hirst. Lastly, there's Operation de Matisse, played just like the classic Operation game you grew up with, but now players carefully extract organs and bones that are recessed into Matisse's *Large Reclining Nude* (1935). Oversize tweezers included. Takes 30 D batteries (not included). The art may be serious, but the fun is pure fun. ***Fine Art Family Fun Pack: $450 million.***

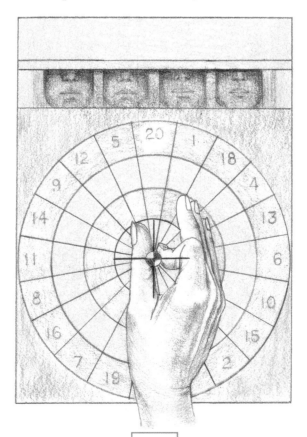

87:1 Scale Model Bavarian Village

In many homes, the centerpiece of the family's Christmas decorations is a miniature (1:87) Bavarian village, a snow-covered idyll complete with tiny villagers arranged in various festive holiday tableaux. In these homes a common wistful utterance is, "I wish I could shrink down and walk around there." If any of this sounds familiar, we have excellent news: Your wish is obsolete. Our 87:1 Scale Model Bavarian Village is an upsized, full-size working replica of your tabletop Christmas creation. Working from faithfully detailed draftings of your holiday display, our expert model makers will acquire sufficient Bundesland acreage and replicate your topography; construct, decorate, and furnish all residential and commercial structures; add any required seasonal touches, like horse-drawn sleighs and lakes for ice-skating and fishing; hire and costume "villagers" to populate the scene during your stay; and top it all off with a thick, even blanket of manufactured snow. This is your chance to walk—and have deed to!—the streets of your dreams. Price varies by the scope and elaborateness of your model village. *87:1 Scale Model Bavarian Village: Call for estimate.*

"The Envy of Omaha" Steaks

Steak lovers need not apply. Steak worshippers? Grab your knives and forks. We start with top-end, genuine Kobe beef: four 10-ounce filets mignons sword-carved by the Butcher to the Emperor's Court from a prudently marbled member of the Imperial Herd. The fresh filets, trimmed to a precise fat-to-flesh ratio, are rushed from abattoir to airport by helicopter, escorted aboard a Gulfstream G550, and flown at Mach .85 to Hilo, Hawaii. In-flight, the steaks are submerged in a marinade of sea salt, fresh ground pepper, cumin, and liquefied oxygen, each scrupulously measured out in a precise and inviolate number of crystals, grains, particles, and molecules, respectively. From Hilo, the meat is raced to the lava fields of Kilauea and flash-seared over a magma flow at 1200° Celsius by the world's sole Cordon Bleu–certified volcanic chef. Their succulent juices conserved within, the warm, rare-cooked filets are placed in a humidity-controlled radiant warming chamber and returned to the refueled Gulfstream for transport to your city, your door. They arrive, once per month, still warm, moist, tender, ready to plate. And the taste? Magma-nificent. *1 year of "The Envy of Omaha" Steaks: $297,000.*

Wild Hair Implants

Though follicly challenged, you've long resisted rugs and plugs. Not because they look like rugs and plugs, but because they're dreary. But that's about to change. Wild Hairs are just what they sound like: implants taken from the planet's most exotic, most colorful, most endangered species and surgically inserted into your scalp. Choose from panda, tiger, leopard, cheetah, zebra, Dalmatian, even Don King. Within weeks, you can have a full head of living, luxurious, thick, fabulous fur. In fabulous patterns, colors, and textures. Each hair, follicle and all, is harvested in the wild, packed in ice, and flown by charter jet to our transplant facility. So hairs are live, fresh, vibrant, and vital. And since our harvest method is cruelty-free, your chances of being spattered with red paint by animal activists is minimized. ***Wild Hair Implants (per square inch): $200,000.***

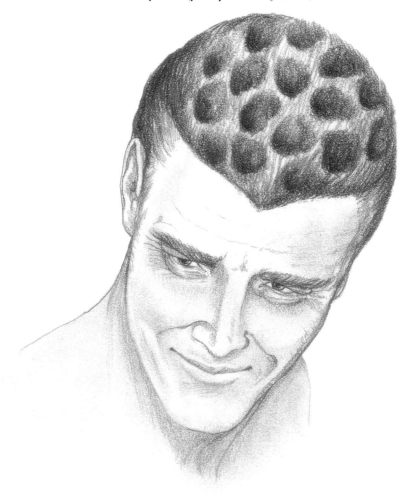

Grampsopoly

Grandfather. Granddad. Grampy. Pop-pop. Whatever you call the man who was your dad's dad (or even your dad's dad's dad), he was definitely "The Man With the Acquisitive Plan." It was he who made the family's fortune by identifying a need, satisfying it, then efficiently eliminating any competition to supply it. If you've ever longed to live your heritage, to return to that simpler, more glorious era, when price-fixing and tightly controlling supply weren't things to hide from the attorney general, but to execute boldly and proudly in full light of day, the game of Grampsopoly is for you. The board is one large space, which, since you own the game, you have deed to from the outset. Play proceeds as each player's game piece circles the board if and when you choose to permit it. Upon passing GO, opponents pay you whatever rent you deem acceptable. It's that simple. Make the only game in town the only game in your house. Grampsopoly board, (tenant) houses, and (fleabag) hotels are all painstakingly crafted by exploited laborers from compressed salt—salt distilled from the sweat of exploited laborers' brows; money is forged from a variety of precious metals and inscribed with your family crest or company logo. ***Grampsopoly (specify Industry Edition, Commodity Edition, or Service Edition): $500,000. Grampsopoly Deluxe Edition (game box and board made exclusively from De Beers diamonds): $50 million.***

His 'n' Her Slaves

Long out of fashion, slaves are defiantly *back*. Imported exclusively for Serfitt & Cloye from politically cloutless emerging nations, these prime-of-life slaves are broken, domesticated, and anxious to serve (average age on delivery: 25). "Shock collar" technology gives one complete (remote) control without the need for adding unsightly high fences or unpredictably cruel guards to your household. "His" Slave cooks, gardens, and has sex, while "Her" Slave lifts, drives, and has sex. (Specify India Ink, Cinnamon Stick, or Eastern Ochre. Call about limited quantities in prestigious Driven Snow.) *His 'n' Her Slaves (pair): $20 million.*

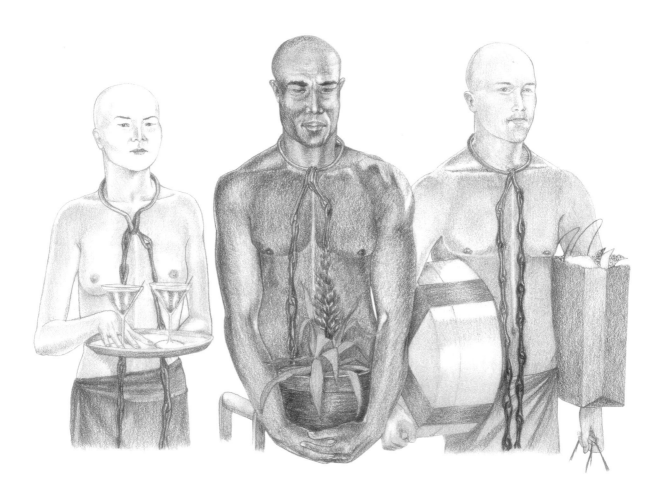

Tri-motorcycle

Mid-life crises come in a variety of flavors, from ennui to infidelity, substance abuse to soldier of fortuneing. The challenge for anyone undergoing one of these difficult periods is, first and foremost, to emerge from it unscathed. For one of this decade's most familiar manifestations of age-related angst, the purchase and riding of motorcycles, the dangers couldn't be more clear and present: An inexperienced operator with (arguably) diminishing reflexes and balance drives a high-power, low-visibility vehicle in heavy, highway-speed traffic or on tortuous rural roadways. Disfigurement or death would seem inevitable. Such a fate is forestalled, however, when one sits astraddle a Tri-motorcycle. Designed and built by America's foremost custom bike fabricator, the Tri-motorcycle is actually a finely balanced trio of custom-chopped Harley Softails discreetly but securely joined in a three-point "flying wing" formation for added stability and visibility. The center or driver's vehicle is flanked by a pair of complementary Harleys that act as "training wheels" that, thanks to their animatronic riders, appear to onlookers as one's biker buddies. Whether for yourself or a loved one, The Tri-motorcycle can prevent a midlife crisis from turning into a medical crisis. Customer's choice of chopper "theme" and animatronic riders' wardrobe (leathers or denim). *Tri-motorcycle: $585,000.*

Media Rare

Thesis: The medium is the message. Fact: A home's media room sends a message. Send yours loudest and clearest. If you haven't updated your electronics since early 2008 or (God forbid) late 2007, now's the time to get up-to-the-moment. Our technicians can transform any space into a media immersion retreat, including the following components: Wall-size Ikegami plasma monitor featuring NHHD (Nature-Humbling High Definition) Digital Color Matrix; Meridian Blu-X-Ray HD-DVR, the only DVD player that makes it possible, with the touch of a button, to electronically remove the clothing of any film's cast; Naim Audio hyperperforming amplifier/preamplifier featuring WaxReader®, an ambient echo-imaging technology that continuously assesses the discrepancy between a listener's left and right earwax accumulation and density, then micro-tweaks the Surround Sound balance accordingly; Wisdom Audio surround speaker cluster, capable of volume levels deemed "bloody excessive" by Ozzy Osbourne; Nintendo GrafXtC 2048-bit gaming console, so deep, so fast, so real, two game testers were killed in a "fall" while skiing its Italian Alps simulator; and more. Put yourself at the epicenter of an audio-visual womb. *Media Rare: $850,000.*

We like radio as much as the next guy, but nary a night around the RCA Victor goes by that we don't think, *Boy oh boy, would pictures help this experience*. We're guessing you think the same thing. Because after so many decades of photo-filled newspapers and illustrated books, the modern human brain expects and craves images with a story. Our Live-In RadiArtist is the answer to your brain's prayer, making radio come alive as he quickly sketches not merely plausible but uncannily accurate pictures of all that you're hearing. You'll plainly see the cacophonous clutter in Fibber McGee's closet, finally get a look at the many deterrents along the way to Jack Benny's safe, and much, much more. So banish those vague, individual, unshared mental images out of your head. See what you're hearing without relying on your unsubstantiated imagination. *Live-In RadiArtist (per year): $15,000. (Room and board not included.)*

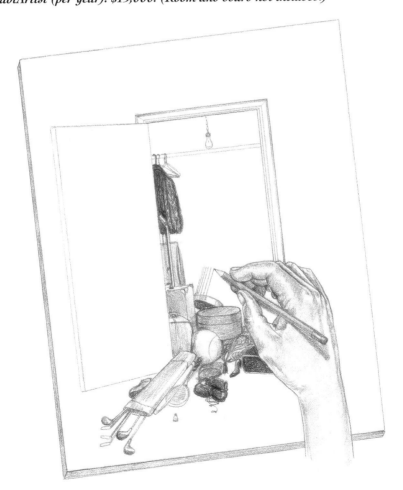

Mammona Archipelago

Vacation should be a time to kick back, stretch out. And here you truly will. Because unlike single private tropical islands, the Mammona Archipelago isn't confining or restricting. Nor does it present you with the problem of staring at the same boring scenery every day. And your secluded space will never be encroached on by the prying eyes or errant outrigger of the native population one island over, because that one is yours, too, and all malingerers have been evicted. As owner of the Mammona Archipelago, you'll have 27 tropical islands—27 individual "rooms"—to call home, to move among freely. You'll sleep on Master Bedroom Island (a short wade from Master Bath Atoll), read on Den Island, relax on Hammock Island, nosh on Kitchen Island, and so much more. Over 400 square acres of living space. Located in the South Pacific (exact coordinates provided upon request), these islands are lush, verdant, and volcanic in origin, each with its own coral-reef lagoon and closely managed schools of exotic tropical fish. Infrastructure—including roads, bridges, docks, et cetera—is in place and of superior construction; can be painted to suit. Updated mechanics, including electricity and intra-archipelagic fresh water plumbing system. *Mammona Archipelago: $1 billion.*

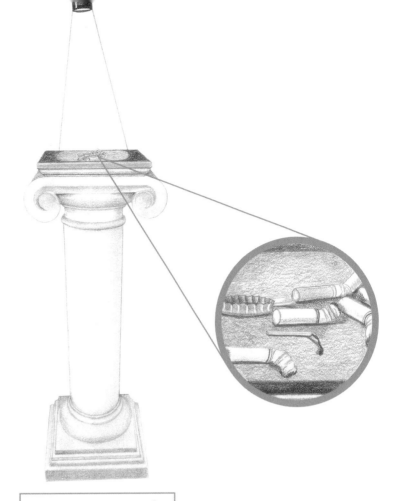

Foe Masterwork

An exceedingly rare opportunity to own a seminal work by ground-breaking sculptress Flair Foe (1956–1992). Foe first came to prominence in the early seventies, around the time of the graffiti movement; unlike Basquiat and Haring, however, she preferred to create three-dimensional art. Her reputation was made when she famously wrote in *Artforum*, "Just as graffiti is not public vandalism but guerilla art, so my work is not littering but, rather, random sculpture." Typically, Foe's works combine the found objects of Dadaism, the pop iconography of Warhol, and the chance procedures of John Cage. Her creations are highly prized and avidly sought by museums and private collectors alike. In 2004, her "Happy Meal Wrapper on Route 27" (1978) sold at auction for $400,000, and in 2005, "Beer Cup and Hot Dog Thrown at Darryl Strawberry" (1987) set a new record for post-sculptural sculpture, commanding $825,000. We offer "Emptied" (1976), a haunting mélange of ashes, cigarette butts, gum wrappers, and a half-finished peppermint candy, which Foe originally installed in a mall parking lot via her car's ashtray. *Foe Masterwork (residing on 6 square feet of excavated parking-lot blacktop and installed in the buyer's home): $1.25 million.*

Some children draw smiling suns; your child draws suns with a joyful visage indicative of a dynamic sense of self. Some children paint crude geometric shapes; your child paints shapes that deconstruct and comment on the concept of geometric shapes. Some children draw stickmen; your child draws stick-figures with a less confining sexuality. These pictures, as well as the ongoing gallery show that is your refrigerator, make one thing very clear: Your child is a gifted genius artist. And what better way to support and encourage this wunderkind than by imposing the work upon the world. Simply select one of his or her tours de force, write a brief description or explanation of its figures, mood, and intent, then send it to us via prepaid, preinsured protective mailer. Next stop, Pixar, the established leader in computer-animated films, where it will be swiftly green-lit for production. After a director and stars have been attached, Pixar will develop a script, bring the images to three-dimensional life, and transform your child's artistic vision into a full-length feature ready for wide release. Boffo! Price includes rave reviews by Gene Shalit and Peter Travers. ***Your Child's Picture in Pictures: $150 million (development and production only); $300 million (with marketing and distribution).***

You in the Moon

Not even Serfitt & Cloye can deliver immortality. (Yet!) But how about the next best thing? How about your likeness looming above the planet in perpetuity? Yes. That we can do. No longer will humankind gaze upon a generic, unknown "Man in the Moon." Now it will be *you* they see. *You* who lights the night sky. *You* who rhymes with "June." By interfacing today's most sophisticated facial mapping techniques with ahead-of-the-curve CAD/CAM software, we will create a detailed computerized blueprint of your every feature. Then, through the deployment of remote-control backhoes, bulldozers, and grading equipment, we will re-contour the craters and seas of the moon in your precise image. King Tut, eat your heart out. (Lunar surface reconfiguration shall not be limited to the face of the purchaser; any person, image, or corporate logo is acceptable.) ***You in the Moon: $50 billion.***

For more fine books from TOW Books and F+W Publications, visit www.tow books.com and www.fwpublications.com.

12 11 10 09 08   5 4 3 2 1

Distributed in Canada by Fraser Direct, 100 Armstrong Avenue, Georgetown, Ontario, Canada L7G 5S4, Tel: (905) 877-4411. Distributed in the U.K. and Europe by David & Charles, Brunel House, Newton Abbot, Devon, TQ12 4PU, England, Tel: (+44) 1626 323200, Fax: (+44) 1626 323319, E-mail: postmaster@ davidandcharles.co.uk. Distributed in Australia by Capricorn Link, P.O. Box 704, Windsor, NSW 2756 Australia, Tel: (02) 4577-3555.

Library of Congress Cataloging-in-Publication Data

Woodiwiss, Bob.
  The Serfitt & Cloye gift catalog : just enough of too much / by Bob Woodiwiss.
-- 1st ed.
      p. cm.
  ISBN 978-1-58297-550-4 (pbk. : alk. paper)
  1. Mail-order business--Humor. 2. Commercial catalogs--Humor. I. Title. II.
Title: Serfitt and Cloye gift catalog.
  PN6231.M17W66 2008
  818'.5402--dc22

                                                                    2008019776

Edited by John Warner and Jane Friedman
Designed by Grace Ring
Illustrated by Andrea Jensen
Production coordinated by Mark Griffin